nF419511

THE SATANIC AIM

of the

United Nations,

World Economic Forum

& Great Reset

"Shall the prey be taken from the mighty, or the lawful captives be delivered? But thus says Yahweh, 'Even the captives of the mighty shall be taken away, and the prey of the terrible shall be delivered; for I will contend with him who contends with you, and I will save your children. I will feed those who oppress you with their own flesh; and they shall be drunken with their own blood, as with sweet wine: and all flesh shall know that I, Yahweh, am your Savior, and your Redeemer, the Mighty One of Jacob.'"

—Isaiah 49:25-26 (WEB)

Table of Contents

Foreword

There is an ancient parable from India that you may have heard before. It recounts a group of blind wise men taking turns to decide, by their sense of touch alone, what exactly an elephant is.

Blind Men and an Elephant

One man feels the tail and says it is like a rope. Another man feels the ear and says it is like a fan. Another feels the leg and describes it as a tree. Another feels the tusk and believes it is like a spear. In the end, none of the men fully comprehends the body of the elephant, each man being able to "see"

Foreword

only separate parts of the whole. Had any of the men done an overall inspection, he would have come to a drastically different conclusion about the behemoth standing before him.

Perception of Conspiracy

When presented with an argument that certain things happening in the world are due to the deliberate and organized efforts of a group of malevolent actors, people can find it hard to accept. Many are inclined to immediately dismiss the very notion as preposterous. I believe the main reason that people tend to reflexively reject such ideas is that they do not see the connections among the supposed perpetrators, their motives and actions.

Concerning allegations of extreme malevolence, there also arises natural doubt that evil of such magnitude could exist in the hearts of human beings, as we tend to think of people as being basically good; especially the leaders we have been conditioned to trust implicitly to safeguard our well-being.

This is part of a passage from Adolph Hitler's, *Mein Kampf,* wherein he reveals his conception of the "big lie" as an effective strategy for deceiving the masses. Despite that he was accusing the Jews of this as he wrote it, history has shown well enough that it was actually he who applied the principle to turn the German people against the Jews:

> *"...in the big lie there is always a certain force of credibility; because the broad masses of a nation are always more easily corrupted in the deeper strata of*

their emotional nature than consciously or voluntarily; and thus in the primitive simplicity of their minds they more readily fall victims to the big lie than the small lie, since they themselves often tell small lies in little matters but would be ashamed to resort to large-scale falsehoods. It would never come into their heads to fabricate colossal untruths, and they would not believe others could have the impudence to distort the truth so infamously. Even though the facts which prove this to be so may be brought clearly to their minds, they will still doubt and waver and will continue to think there may be some other explanation."[1]

It is fair-minded to assume positive intent in the actions of others, unless you have some good reason not to. So, it is reasonable that we would want to see evidence that a sinister motive, unity of purpose and intention really exist before we begin suspecting others' words and deeds as conspiratorial. I believe that a secondary reason for the reticence of most people to even consider such possibilities is that the popular interpretation of the term "conspiracy" has, over time, had a connotation of absurdity attached to it. The word "conspiracy" comes from Latin roots suggestive of "breathing together" or "together in spirit". It refers to a group of people colluding, usually secretly, to achieve a common selfish objective. In today's world —especially in the news media— the lone word "conspiracy" is broadly and quite incorrectly tossed back and forth as a sort of shorthand for "conspiracy theory". In turn, "conspiracy theory" is often used fallaciously as a label meant to damn to the realm of the irrational any notion of people conspiring to achieve a nefarious goal, as though this were a non-existent phenomenon.

In the real world, though, men have been known to conspire against others since the dawn of time, and a theory is simply an idea about something that remains to be demonstrated as fact. Any theory of any kind should be judged on its merits.

I suspect that a shift in the perception of that word may have been deliberately made, in psychology texts, for example, by those who have had the influence to do so and wished to see it disappear from the vocabulary of serious inquiry. After all, would it not benefit the planners of the greatest conspiracies against mankind to convince its victims that ideas of conspiracies were the fantasies of overactive minds or signs of mental illness?

As one old saying goes, "The best trick the devil ever pulled was to persuade the world that he didn't exist".

If we abandon all common sense and pretend to be unaware of the ways in which greed and power can corrupt the thoughts and actions of men, then we might be able to delude ourselves into thinking that people abruptly ceased all organized plotting of evil schemes after some climactic instance in history which was the final one; that all organized crimes against humanity that have occurred since then have been just unplanned, spontaneous events. Otherwise, as long as we maintain a firm grip on reality, we should still keep an open mind and a watchful eye.

In this world, absolute proof of anything is elusive, and anything one person holds up as proof could somehow be deemed meaningless by another. What is still relevant, though, is the significance of evidence to the minds of most rational people. The more compelling the evidence is in the perception of the observer, the closer to proof it is regarded.

I want to be clear that, in these pages, I am not professing to show proof but rather attempting to show an interconnected body of evidence which points to the conclusion that we, the majority of the human race, are being targeted in a concerted, malevolent aim.

Although I believe this threat is originally and ultimately spiritual in nature and is ancient, I feel that, since 2019, it has been manifesting in the physical world more acutely, pervasively and rapidly than most of us alive today have ever experienced. Although I have no aspiration of being able to see the bigger picture in all of its complex detail, I will attempt to draw a clear enough outline of the beast that stands before us so that you might recognize it as I do.

The Spiritual Impulse behind the United Nations

In the late 1960s, American writer and theatrical producer, Myron Fagan, claimed that the United Nations was the "crux of the great conspiracy to destroy the sovereignty of the United States" in his audio exposé entitled *Illuminati C.F.R.* His story began all the way back at the formation of the Order of the Illuminati by Adam Weishaupt in the 1760s with the backing of Mayer Rothschild, and the various names and guises that it has subsequently operated under —including Freemasonry— during the course of its slow march toward world domination.[2]

As for the Illuminati, despite having been mystified in popular fiction over the years, there is nothing paranormal about its story that we should see it catalogued with myths and legends. Adam Weishaupt certainly modeled his Illuminist organization after other prominent secret societies of the time — such as Freemasonry and the Rosicrucian Order — that claimed heritage to ancient Egyptian mystery cults which had stewarded bodies of arcane knowledge down through the millennia, and he embellished Illuminism with the same sort of allegory and esoteric symbolism that lent it such an appearance. [3][4]

Adam Weishaupt (1748-1830)

by Friedrich Rossmassler, 1799 - From Unknown source., Public Domain

Although there are reports that he had travelled to Egypt and studied eastern religions and mysticism for a few years before he established his Order of the Illuminati,[5] it is hard to say whether Weishaupt was more a devotee of spiritualism or a power-hungry opportunist leveraging the impression of being one in order to attract supporters at a time when fraternal societies — the more enigmatic the better — were in vogue among hobnobbing affluents. However, that is not to deny that his agenda was diabolically inspired.

Weishaupt's plan to subjugate humanity under the pretense of liberating the common man from enslavement by evil despots was devised and set in motion in an era that was marked by social unrest and primed for revolutions which he undoubtedly saw as an opportune moment. So strikingly similar is Illuminism in its basic principles to what we recognize as communism today, that it is reasonable to guess that it was used as the template for the Marxist doctrine drawn up many decades later. To illustrate this, Weishaupt's seven-part plan for Illuminism was as follows:

> 1. Abolition of all Ordered Governments
>
> 2. Abolition of Private Property
>
> 3. Abolition of Inheritance
>
> 4. Abolition of Patriotism
>
> 5. Abolition of the Family Unit
>
> 6. Abolition of Religion
>
> 7. Creation of a New World Order (World Government)[6]

I recommend listening to Fagan's presentation for his rich insights into the shady and intricate history of the affair from the inception of the Illuminati through to the late 1960s. My starting point within this timeline is more recent, though, with a focus on the spiritual orientation of the United Nations, those who claim to be directing it, and the progression of related developments which have become increasingly overt and personally impactful on ordinary people into 2022.

Since its foundation in 1922 by one Alice Bailey, the organization named the Lucis Trust has served as the supporting platform for the publication of her series of twenty-four books of esoteric philosophy as well as other endeavors including the establishment of the occult Arcane School, *The Beacon* magazine, a program involving group meditation called Triangles, and the World Goodwill organization.[7]

Bailey was deeply immersed in occultism, having been an avid scholar of Theosophy, and was an inspirator of the New Age movement. Bailey and the Lucis Trust have maintained that she only cooperated in authoring her written works containing the teachings of one she identified as Master Djwhal Khul, a member of a purported group of "Ancient Masters of Wisdom" whom she frequently referred to as "The Tibetan Master", a non-corporeal entity whose messages she claimed to have received via spirit channeling.[8]

Alice Bailey

by Unknown photographer - From Вячеслав Федин., Public Domain

The Theosophical Society, whose teachings Bailey espoused, was co-founded in 1875 by Helena Blavatsky, who also claimed such a connection with the Ancient Masters.[9] [10]

Helena Petrovna Blavatsky (1831-1891)

by Unknown photographer, 1889, London - From Журнал "Культура и время".,
Public Domain

Revealing a crucial tenet of the Theosophical belief system, is this passage from Blavatsky's book, The Secret Doctrine:

> *"It is 'Satan who is the god of our planet and the only god,' and this without any allusive metaphor to its wickedness and depravity."*[11] [12] [13]

In case anyone might think that this was taken out of context, be aware that Lucis Trust points out that "in 1887 the magazine of the Theosophical Society took 'Lucifer' as its name in an effort to bring clarity to what it regarded as an unfairly maligned sacrificing angel".[14]

Similarly, the publishing house that Alice Bailey and her husband, Foster Bailey, set up under the umbrella of the Lucis Trust was originally named Lucifer Publishing Company until the name was changed a few years later.

Today, the Lucis Trust offers the explanation that Bailey and her husband "like the great teacher H.P. Blavatsky, for whom they had enormous respect, sought to elicit a deeper understanding of the sacrifice made by Lucifer"[15] (which refers to the "fall" from his position in the heavens in order to grant the gift of illumination to the minds of human beings).

In their spiritual philosophy, Lucifer was a liberating hero of humanity and God was an oppressive tyrant who sought to prevent mankind from achieving true awareness and reaching its full potential. Given that Lucifer is venerated in the belief system that it promotes, the imperatives of the Lucis Trust and those who are in league with it would wisely be regarded as Satanically inspired.

> *"And the great dragon was thrown down, that ancient serpent, who is called the devil and Satan, the deceiver of the whole world —he was thrown down to the earth, and his angels were thrown down with him."*

—Revelation 12:9 (ESV)

The Luciferians' story of Satan both starkly contrasts and closely parallels the historic account found within Judeo-Christian scriptures of the banishment of Lucifer —along with a cohort of other rebellious angels that he brought down with him— from the heaven where God dwells, as the consequence of his prideful defiance of God's sovereignty and his jealous loathing for His creation of humankind. Lucifer transmitted forbidden knowledge to the first generation of humans which they accepted in defiance of God's commandment, and this, similarly, led to their own egoism, loss of innocence and expulsion from what had been a state of perfect harmony with God in His immediate presence.

I believe that the Luciferian twist on Satan as a benevolent entity is a strategy designed to appeal to those who lack the spiritual grounding to avoid being duped into accepting a reversal in polarity of the nature of the devil from that which has been commonly known by the Abrahamic religions for thousands of years.

Christians understand that Lucifer and Satan are two names of the same spiritual entity —the adversary of God— and reject both the claims of Luciferian spiritualists that he retains his original virtuous nature as a holy angel and the claims of Satanic atheists that he does not actually exist other than as a symbolic figure. We are also aware that the devil is notoriously deceptive and achieves his purpose simply by causing a person to turn away from God; a person's belief in his existence being irrelevant to his success.

The number of followers of modern organized Satanism —atheistic, as the Satanic Church and Temple both profess the religion to be—[16] [17] would be naturally limited to those that could be gathered from among the imaginably small subset of people who reject the notion of the supernatural but would still be comfortable chanting "Hail Satan", engaging in religious rites and rituals even including human sacrifice.[18] So, it does make sense that, for Satan's following to continue to grow, another angle was used: portraying Satan in a positive, spiritual light... as he is in Luciferian Theosophy.

Cloaked in brilliance, declaring unity, peace and goodwill toward all, promising the elevation of humanity to greater heights of wisdom —a deceptively Christlike figure— the freshly rebranded image of Lucifer would be hard to resist for many who are well-meaning yet spiritually misguided. For the Father of Lies, that the truth of his sinister aims will eventually be discovered by his New Age followers would presumably not matter, as the number of souls led into ruin in the end will have justified the means of their recruitment.

For many decades, the United Nations has been — you might say — courted by the Lucis Trust, which enjoys consultative status with the Economic and Social Council of the UN[19] that allows it to take part in formal deliberations. Its U.S. headquarters is conveniently located at United Nations Plaza.[20] Unsurprisingly, another of its three global offices is located in Geneva, Switzerland, which is where one of the four UN offices and the headquarters of the World Economic Forum are both also situated.[21] [22]

The founder and president of the Aquarian Age Community, Dr. Ida Urso, who also happens to have been the director of the Lucis Trust's World Goodwill organization[23] gave a speech in 1995 at a conference of the Lucis Trust's Arcane School entitled, *Let Purpose Guide the Little Wills of Men: The Spiritual Impulse Behind the United Nations*, wherein she framed the role of the United Nations within the context of the Theosophical world view and concluded her presentation with a statement about the destiny of the UN quoted from *The Externalisation of the Hierarchy*, one of the books of Alice Bailey.[24]

In her writings, Bailey mentioned the United Nations repeatedly and stressed the critical role that the UN will play, when it "emerge[s] into factual and actual power",[25] in bringing about a new world religion to complement the New World Order:

> *"Thus the expressed aims and efforts of the United Nations will be eventually brought to fruition and a new church of God, gathered out of all religions and spiritual groups, will unitedly bring to an end the great heresy of separateness."*[26]

Although the Lucis Trust's formal connection is acknowledged by the UN in its online database of consultative NGOs[27] —which is no small group, mind you— the manner and extent that Lucis Trust engages with the UN is not elaborated on there. It is, however, detailed on Lucis Trust's website, on its page entitled "Support of the United Nations".[28]

According to Lucis Trust, its World Goodwill organization —which seeks to apply the Theosophical teachings of its Arcane School in addressing global problems— has been organizing regular monthly meditation sessions at the United Nations for decades since the tradition was started by "a number of spiritually oriented co-workers of the UN in Geneva".[29]

World Goodwill is also on the council of the Spiritual Caucus at the United Nations, a group of spiritually-oriented NGOs which holds regular meetings at the UN's headquarters in New York for meditation, the sharing of insights and exploration of ways of using inner focus in service to the work of the UN to "balance and strengthen the endeavors of the UN system and its affiliates".[30] Both Lucis Trust and World Goodwill are listed as members of the NGO Forum on Spirituality and Values of the NGO Alliance on Global Concerns "for an efficient NGO engagement with the United Nations"[31]

Lucis Trust's web page for its World Goodwill organization practically showers praise on the United Nations and begs people to focus their meditative energies and prayers on it, send donations to it, talk about it, learn about it, teach about it, etc.[32] On its "Worldwide Network: Units of Service" web page, it recommends "informing the public of the principles and programmes of the United Nations, a major externalised focal point of the energy of goodwill" as an activity in the same list and apparently of the same level of priority as "distributing the Great Invocation, a world prayer" and "forming [meditative] triangles of light and goodwill".[33] This all goes to show the faith they place in the UN as the shining star of hope for the realization of their cause.

The UN's observance of the annual World Interfaith Harmony Week,[34] not surprisingly, appears to be on track with Alice Bailey's prophesy of a new world religion which has been carried forward by

Lucis Trust and World Goodwill. Lucis Trust's own assessment of World Interfaith Harmony Week, while lamenting that it does not encompass the three fundamental truths at the core of its envisioned new world religion, is that it is a platform bringing together many faiths and inter-faith groups and thus still provides "a basis to build upon".[35] For them, the UN is *a work in progress.*

Although the Lucis Trust and its various programs are very clear about their directing of spiritual energies of "goodwill" at the United Nations, reliable accounts of their people physically meeting with UN personnel are difficult to find. I suspect that this might be intentionally so, considering the Lucis Trust's controversial occultist worldview in contrast to the UN's need to keep up an appearance of universal neutrality. However, for what it's worth, in 1962, there was an article entitled "Between the Lines: The Universal Theocratic State" written by Edith Kermit Roosevelt in the New Hampshire Sunday Times News, wherein she reported that "Recognizing the 'goofy network' to be a source of power and influence, UN officials lecture at meetings of the Arcane School, the international 'group of New World Servers,' who form 'Triangles' to work for UNESCO."[36] Recall that the Arcane School and Triangles are projects of the Lucis Trust, and know that the "New World Servers" is the name of their worldwide network of individuals and organizations who have committed to disseminating their Theosophical teachings and participating in prescribed "triangle" group meditation sessions to target their spiritual energies.[37][38]

In Alice Bailey's book, *The Destiny of the Nations,* published in 1949, she delineated what she called three "planetary centers" from which emanate the spiritual impulses that correspond to the three aspects of the nature of God, giving the name and related concepts for each, as follow:

1. Shamballa	Will or Power	Planetary Head Centre	Ruler: **Sanat** Kumara, the **Lord of the World**
2. The Hierarchy	Love-Wisdom	Planetary Heart Centre	Ruler: **The Christ**
3. Humanity	Active Intelligence	Planetary Throat Centre	Ruler: **Lucifer**[39]

Keeping in mind that Bailey had mentioned the "Lord of the World" in her writings as early as 1922, namely in *Letters On Occult Meditation*, it is curious that *Lord of the World* was also the title of a dystopian novel that had been published fifteen years earlier by Catholic Monsignor Robert Hugh Benson that told of the rise of a unified world system of governance under the Antichrist, to whom his title refers.

Despite that the story was a work of fiction, it has recently been upheld —for better or worse— by two successive *Popes* as being a potentially accurate forecast of how future events might unfold through the establishment of a New World Order.[40]

Even if we dismiss as pure coincidence the existence of a book of the same name referring to the Antichrist not long before Alice Bailey's writings began, and we take it for granted that Bailey was unaware of it, the term "Lord of the World" is still undeniably reminiscent of various terms found in the New Testament of the Bible, including "Ruler of this world" (John 12:31, 14:30, & 16:11) and "God of this world" (2 Corinthians 4:4), that are well-known references to Satan. As accustomed as she was to quoting passages from scripture, there is no reason to doubt that Bailey was aware of this.

One is then reasonably inclined to wonder whether the name "Sanat", the entity whom Bailey named as "Lord of the World", was actually an anagram for "Satan" If she meant to so obscure her reference to Satan, then her overtness in having named "Lucifer" as the "ruler" of an aspect of the nature of God is puzzling, even if the fact that she named him is not surprising.

Original book cover of
Lord of the World
by Robert Hugh Benson

by Unknown illustrator 1907 - From
L.W. Currey, Inc., Public Domain

As for Bailey's mention of "the Christ" which Christians will know is entirely misplaced between the first and third so-called "rulers" as perceived above, note that she used this term extensively throughout her esoteric philosophy. There are no less than 167 occurrences of "Christ" found in an open-text search of her books on the Lucis Trust website, as well as 33 instances of "Jesus".[41]

Although these two names featured prominently in Bailey's spiritual philosophy, it becomes apparent from even cursory reading that Bailey was *not* describing the same *Jesus* Christ that Christians recognize as the Son of God.

To illustrate this point, here is a statement from Bailey's book, *Rays and the Initiations*, by which she clearly distinguished "Master Jesus" and "the Christ" as separate personalities:

> *"The second, and much the most important rent*, was made by the power of the second aspect when the Christ subjected the Master Jesus to the fourth initiation and Their joint influence was triumphant over death.*[emphasis added]" [42]

> * an apparent reference to the rending of the temple veil, cf. Matthew 27:51

This further clarifies that, as "the Christ" in Bailey's mind was not perpetually one in the same as Jesus the son of Mary, she must have esteemed someone else as the coming messiah.

Bailey wrote of divine energies of distinctly varying characters that affect the disposition and destiny of mankind, which she called "rays". Two such rays that she claimed have a particularly powerful influence over mankind during the present era are the *waning* 6th Ray "of Abstract Devotion or Idealism" and the *waxing* 7th Ray "of Ceremonial Magic or Organisation". To examine the significance that Bailey attributed to these, let us review a couple of passages from her book, *The Destiny of the Nations*:

> *"Suffice it to say that the sixth ray people are the reactionaries, the conservatives, the die-hards and the fanatics, who hold on to all that is of the past and whose influence is potent to hinder the progress of humanity into the new age. Their name is legion. They provide, however, a needed balance and are responsible for a steadying process which is much*

needed in the world at this time.[emphasis added]"
43

In the above passage, Bailey characterized those who maintain conservative, traditional values as an obstacle to the spiritual evolution of humanity. She took a passive-aggressive stab at such people, effectively equating them with "unclean spirits", by stating "Their name is legion".

For those who do not recognize it: This was a veiled Biblical reference to the collective response given to Jesus by a host of demons inhabiting a man when —in the course of the exorcism— Jesus asked what the demon's name was. They replied "My (Our) name is Legion, for we are many" (Mark 5:9). Bailey then implied that such people are, even so, a necessary evil —at least for the time being— for the stabilizing purpose they serve.

> *"The seventh ray is steadily gaining momentum and has for a long time been stimulating and enhancing the activity of all fifth ray nations. If you bear in mind that one of the major objectives of seventh ray energy is to bring together and to relate spirit and matter and also substance and form (note this distinction) you can see for yourself that the work of science is closely connected with this endeavour and that the creation of the new forms will definitely be the result of a working interaction between the rulers of the fifth, the second and the seventh rays, aided by the help —on demand— of the ruler of the first ray. A large number of seventh ray egos or souls and also of men and women with seventh ray personalities are coming into incarnation now, and to them is committed the task of organising the activities of the new era and of ending the old methods of life and the old crystallised attitudes to life, to death, to leisure and to the population."*44

To explain the above passage: Bailey asserted that the growing influence of ceremonial magic or organization (the 7th ray) has been driving scientifically-advanced nations (the 5th ray) toward achieving the goal of synthesizing human spirit, matter, substance and form into new life forms, and that this will be accomplished with the cooperation of "Christ's ray" (which is the 2nd ray) and of government (the 1st ray) wherever necessary.

Now, although Bailey did not specifically state that the "new forms" to be created will be new forms of *human life*, this can be inferred: She said that new physical forms would be created through scientific advancements and would incorporate *spirit*. That she did mean new *human* life forms will become all the more evident when we examine, in just a moment, exactly how this prophesy is being realized today.

Bailey went on to say that both spiritual entities and people who are heavily influenced by the energy of ceremonial magic or organization (characterized by the so-called 7th ray) are increasingly emerging on the earth for the purpose of bringing to an end traditional ways of living (and/or the conventional means of progenerating life) and customary perspectives on life, death, leisure and the population in order to usher in the New Age.[45]

At present, there is no clearer manifestation of Bailey's prophesy of scientific advancement toward the creation of new forms of life and the concomitant *redefinition of life and death* than the movement of transhumanism, of which the most openly vocal proponent today is the World Economic Forum (WEF).[46]

The WEF also happens to have a formal alliance with the UN for the expressed purpose of advancing the UN's objectives. In June 2019, the two organizations entered into a "Strategic Partnership Framework outlining areas of cooperation to deepen institutional engagement and jointly accelerate the implementation of the 2030 Agenda for Sustainable Development."[47]

The WEF seeks to realize, through its trademark "Great Reset" agenda,[48] what it calls *The Fourth Industrial Revolution* described by the WEF's founder, Klaus Schwab, in his 2017 book of that title. The WEF states that...

> "[*The Fourth Industrial Revolution*] *is characterized by a range of new technologies that are fusing the physical, digital and biological worlds, impacting all disciplines, economies and industries, and even challenging ideas about what it means to be human.*"[49]

Once again, reflect back on Alice Bailey's foretelling of the ending of crystallised attitudes toward life and death. The WEF paints an even clearer picture of the impact on human beings, when it states...

> "*Emerging technologies, particularly in the biological realm, are also raising new questions about what it means to be human. The Fourth Industrial Revolution is the first where the tools of technology can become literally embedded within us and even purposefully change who we are at the level of our genetic makeup. It is completely conceivable that forms of radical human improvement will be available within a generation, innovations that risk creating entirely new forms of inequality and class conflict.*"[49B]

At this point, there should be no question in your mind that the WEF, through the scientific means of biodigital convergence and genetic engineering, intends for the creation of new types of human life so far beyond natural man that they will be regarded as a superior class. This is in line with Alice Bailey's Luciferian prophesy.

The WEF proposes medical procedures including neuro-technological brain enhancements and genetic editing as potential means to that end. Considering that most of the novel vaccines are effectively gene-therapies[50] [50B] [50C] and that they contain nanoparticles[51], one could speculate that they may be (or be a prototype of) a combinative medium —a sort of *transmission fluid*, if you will— in this process of fusing human biology with technology.

"The merging of our physical, our digital and our biological identity", as Schwab phrased it in his talk at the Chicago Council on Global Affairs in May 2019,[52] literally means augmenting the brains and bodies of human beings —possibly even in combination with non-living objects— with digital technology. This has been termed "biodigital convergence".[53]

If this sounds implausible, consider that Elon Musk's enterprise, NeuraLink, is reportedly nearly ready to implant microchips into human brains.[54]

Several years ago, Bill Gates' company, Microsoft, registered a patent for a process of generating digital currency from the energy produced from human bodily activity, which the patent's description says could be achieved by connecting a computer to a person using a brainwave-monitoring MRI device. Curiously, the patent number is "0**60606**",[55] eerily reminiscent of the number of The Beast:

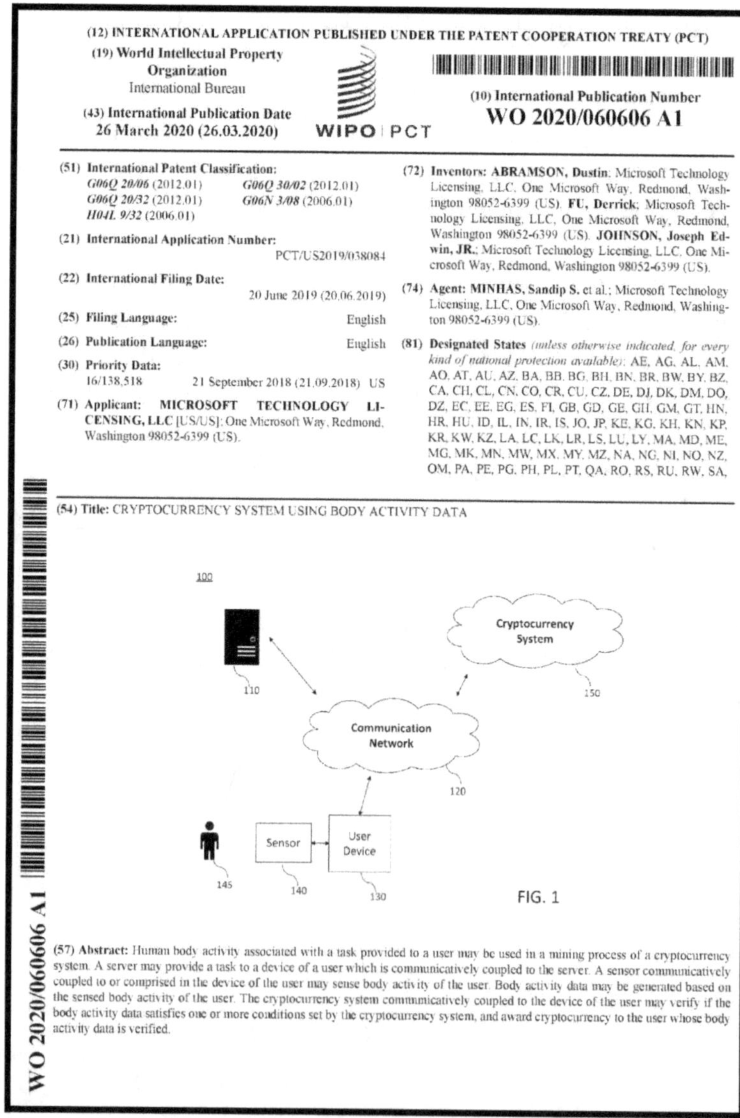

(12) INTERNATIONAL APPLICATION PUBLISHED UNDER THE PATENT COOPERATION TREATY (PCT)

(19) World Intellectual Property Organization
International Bureau

(43) International Publication Date
26 March 2020 (26.03.2020)

WIPO | PCT

(10) International Publication Number
WO 2020/060606 A1

(51) International Patent Classification:
G06Q 20/06 (2012.01) *G06Q 30/02* (2012.01)
G06Q 20/32 (2012.01) *G06N 3/08* (2006.01)
H04L 9/32 (2006.01)

(21) International Application Number:
PCT/US2019/038084

(22) International Filing Date:
20 June 2019 (20.06.2019)

(25) Filing Language: English

(26) Publication Language: English

(30) Priority Data:
16/138,518   21 September 2018 (21.09.2018) US

(71) Applicant: **MICROSOFT TECHNOLOGY LICENSING, LLC** [US/US]: One Microsoft Way, Redmond, Washington 98052-6399 (US).

(72) Inventors: **ABRAMSON, Dustin**: Microsoft Technology Licensing, LLC, One Microsoft Way, Redmond, Washington 98052-6399 (US). **FU, Derrick**; Microsoft Technology Licensing, LLC, One Microsoft Way, Redmond, Washington 98052-6399 (US). **JOHNSON, Joseph Edwin, JR.**; Microsoft Technology Licensing, LLC, One Microsoft Way, Redmond, Washington 98052-6399 (US).

(74) Agent: **MINHAS, Sandip S.** et al.; Microsoft Technology Licensing, LLC, One Microsoft Way, Redmond, Washington 98052-6399 (US).

(81) Designated States *(unless otherwise indicated, for every kind of national protection available)*: AE, AG, AL, AM, AO, AT, AU, AZ, BA, BB, BG, BH, BN, BR, BW, BY, BZ, CA, CH, CL, CN, CO, CR, CU, CZ, DE, DJ, DK, DM, DO, DZ, EC, EE, EG, ES, FI, GB, GD, GE, GH, GM, GT, HN, HR, HU, ID, IL, IN, IR, IS, JO, JP, KE, KG, KH, KN, KP, KR, KW, KZ, LA, LC, LK, LR, LS, LU, LY, MA, MD, ME, MG, MK, MN, MW, MX, MY, MZ, NA, NG, NI, NO, NZ, OM, PA, PE, PG, PH, PL, PT, QA, RO, RS, RU, RW, SA,

(54) Title: CRYPTOCURRENCY SYSTEM USING BODY ACTIVITY DATA

(57) **Abstract:** Human body activity associated with a task provided to a user may be used in a mining process of a cryptocurrency system. A server may provide a task to a device of a user which is communicatively coupled to the server. A sensor communicatively coupled to or comprised in the device of the user may sense body activity of the user. Body activity data may be generated based on the sensed body activity of the user. The cryptocurrency system communicatively coupled to the device of the user may verify if the body activity data satisfies one or more conditions set by the cryptocurrency system, and award cryptocurrency to the user whose body activity data is verified.

WO 2020/060606 A1

Imagine that Mark Zuckerberg's Metaverse, a digital virtual world where one can pretend one's life away,[56] might one day become the overriding reality for those who submit to being digitally converged.

These concepts are no longer the stuff of science-fiction fantasy. These are real things that very rich, powerful and opportunistic people are making happen, supposedly for the wellbeing of mankind. Although these technologies may gather favor among the public by being marketed from humanitarian angles, such as the restoration of functions to those who suffer from disabling conditions, which no one could reject as an honorable objective, Klaus Schwab's wish for biodigital convergence does not seem to be for the benefit of any particular subgroup of the population; he speaks in general terms. His angle seems to be more about making people smarter and more productive, which just so happen to be ideal criteria for an efficient workforce.

To get a vivid mental image of what biodigital convergence might look like if allowed to permeate our lives to the extent that the WEF hopes it will, look no further than the scenarios for the future being proposed by the policy-foresight agency of the Government of Canada, which is quite earnestly exploring the potential applications of biodigital convergence to society.

The February 2020 white paper issued by that agency, Policy Horizons Canada, entitled "Exploring Biodigital Convergence" breaches the topic with phraseology mirroring that used by the WEF and then nonchalantly drops the following bombshell:

> *"Robots with biological brains and biological bodies with digital brains already exist, as do human-computer and brain-machine interfaces. The medical*

use of digital devices in humans, as well as digitally manipulated insects such as drone dragonflies and surveillance locusts, are examples of digital technology being combined with biological entities. By tapping into the nervous system and manipulating neurons, tech can be added to an organism to alter its function and purpose. New human bodies and new senses of identity could arise as the convergence continues."

The paper also mentions a few other new forms of "life", including partly biological furniture and houses that grow. The point in this literature that is, perhaps, what the average person will find the most disturbing is where it suggests that this new paradigm will demand that people alter their perceptions of what is alive and what is not.[57]

This prospect of dabbling with forms and perceptions of life raises a theological question: How much tolerance does *God* have for the alteration of *His* original design for human beings before he ceases to acknowledge a person as one?

Knowing who the scientists are, one should seriously consider whether exceeding His tolerance might be precisely the goal of the experiment. On this point, once again, recall Alice Bailey's foretelling of the ending of crystallised attitudes toward life and death once these new life forms are brought into existence.

This is a clear sign that the Canadian government, for one, is working to align its future policies with the WEF's goal of transhumanising mankind to fulfill the dream of the Luciferian occultists who guide the hand of the UN. This would not be unexpected, given that Canada's Prime Minister, Justin Trudeau, was a WEF protégé, having been groomed to champion its cause during his time as a member of the organization's "Young Global Leaders" (YGL) program —just as *too many* of the world's current leaders and influencers of government, enterprise, academia and mass media have also been.

In fact, the founder of the WEF, Klaus Schwab, confirmed both the influence over the Canadian government that his organization had already established and the WEF's ongoing program of deploying its Young Global Leaders to *infiltrate the decision-making bodies of national governments* when, during a filmed discussion with David R. Gergen at the John F. Kennedy School of Government at Harvard in September 2017, he said:

> "*When I mention, now, names like Mrs. Merkel, even Vladimir Putin, and so on: they all have been Young Global Leaders of the World Economic Forum. But, what we are very proud of now, with the young generation, like Prime Minister Trudeau, President of Argentina, and so on is that we penetrate the cabinets. So, yesterday I was at the reception for Prime Minister Trudeau, and I would know [sic] that half of this cabinet, or even more [than] half of this cabinet are...for our...actually Young Global Leaders of the World Economic Forum.*" [58]

The WEF selects individuals for its YGL program who are under forty years old, have already established themselves in positions of leadership and "are willing to devote their energy and expertise for five years to tackle the most critical issues facing the world."[59] In 2005, the year that the new YGL group was created, its nomination committee was chaired by Queen Rania of Jordan and was, interestingly, comprised entirely of highly influential figures in mass media including Steve Forbes, CEO James R. Murdoch of British Sky Broadcasting Group, CEO Robert C. Wright of NBC, as well as executives of the New York Times, Newsweek, Yahoo!, The Daily Mail and Reuters, just to name a few.[60] This is presumably because the media plays such a crucial role in popularizing these individuals and their viewpoints.

In 2005, the first members of the Young Global Leaders were implored to engage in the "2020 Initiative" and form task forces "on priority issues and develop global and regional strategies, concrete actions and measurable benchmarks" to advance "a shared vision of the world in 2020".[61] In retrospect, it comes as no surprise that, on the 2020 Initiative's topic of "Health in 2020", the very first bullet point in the list of "Examples of challenges and opportunities" was "*Communicable diseases, outbreaks and pandemics*".[62]

A directory of the names, photos and professional titles of members of the WEF's YGL Alumni Network is found on the group's website. There are entries for some very notable people, including French president Emmanuel Macron and Facebook/Meta CEO Mark Zuckerberg.[63] [64] However, this is not a comprehensive list of alumni, as it only goes as far back as 2016, and, as YGL graduates need to proactively register themselves in order to be displayed as members of the group, naturally not all of them would. The YGL website claims a total of over 1,400 active members and alumni combined.[65]

In fact, after having extensively researched the archived official WEF lists of honorees to identify the members of this group going back to its origin in 1993 when it was named "Global Leaders for Tomorrow" (GLT)[66] I have unearthed over 3,500 alumni throughout the world, including some of the individuals whom Klaus Schwab named in 2017 as previous members, such as Angela Merkel. I should mention, though, that —despite Schwab's having mentioned their names as former members— Vladimir Putin and the "President of Argentina" (who was, at that time, Mauricio Macri) did not appear in the lists of honorees.

The number of these people who hold influential positions in national governments, large corporations, media outlets and universities is astounding.

By comparison, the WEF's Global Shapers Community, "a network of young people driving dialogue, action and change" which is to train its future agents of global influence in the one-decade younger age bracket, touts vastly more impressive numbers: over 10,200 active and 4,100 alumni members, with 457 "hubs" located in 148 countries.[67] Active membership in the group appears to have nearly doubled since January 2016, based on a briefing published by the European Parliamentary Research Service which stated that there were 5,300 members at that time.[68] Similar to that for the Young Global Leaders Alumni Network, a directory of the names and photos of registered members of the Global Shapers Alumni Network is accessible on its website.[69]

While examining the shared goals of the UN and the WEF, it is pertinent to reflect on the tenets of Marxism, as they have apparently embraced them as guiding principles. This can be seen at various points in the WEF's literature. As stated on its website "...rethinking capitalism, or giving capitalism a "Great Reset" as WEF Chairman Klaus Schwab has clarified, means that capitalism and socialism will need to merge to create a productive and inclusive economic and social model."[70] So, the WEF is prescribing a higher dose of socialism as the cure for the world's economic and social ills.

In November 2016, on the Twitter social media platform, the WEF released a short video entitled "8 predictions for the world in 2030". Although the video was not well received by the Twitter community, in general, provoked many viewers to leave negative comments and was deleted some days thereafter, it is still viewable on the WEF website. The first, and most infamous, "prediction" declared in the video was "You'll own nothing and you'll be happy" then qualified by "Whatever you want, you'll rent, and it'll be delivered by drone". [71]

With that in mind, let us now reflect on what Karl Marx and Friedrich Engels had to say about property ownership in the *Manifesto of the Communist Party*:

> *"The distinguishing feature of Communism is not the abolition of property generally, but the abolition of bourgeois property. But modern bourgeois private property is the final and most complete expression of the system of producing and appropriating products, that is based on class antagonisms, on the exploitation of the many by the few. In this sense, the theory of the Communists may be summed up in the single sentence:* <u>*Abolition of private property*</u>*.*[emphasis added]"[72]

The parallel of the WEF's notion that private property will cease to exist to Marxism's avowal of it as a cornerstone of communist ideology is impossible to ignore. In fairness, though, do note that "Abolishment of private property" had, as mentioned previously, been decreed *over seventy years earlier* by Adam Weishaupt as one of his seven goals of Illuminism.

The web page on the WEF website where the video is posted explains that the "predictions" were elicited from experts from its various Global Future Councils after they were asked what they thought the world would be like in 2030. This page also offers an elaboration of the underlying rationale for each curtly stated prediction in the video, including a link to a separate WEF-hosted article relevant to each.[73] The linked page there containing the article underlying the "You'll own nothing" prediction no longer exists.

However, that article —actually a futuristic short story entitled "Welcome To 2030: I Own Nothing, Have No Privacy And Life Has Never Been Better", written by Ida Auken, a member of Danish Parliament and of the WEF's "Young Global Leaders" program— was also published on Forbes.com by the WEF on November 10, 2016 and can still be read there.[74] (Do recall that Steve Forbes sat on the Young Global Leaders nomination committee).

As far as offering a meaningful explanation for why we will own nothing by 2030, Auken's utopian story only says that a breakthrough in the harnessing of, and transition to, clean energy will trigger such drastic reductions in the costs of communications, transportation, and gradually everything else —including food, clothing and even housing— that it will all ultimately become free and so there will no longer be any need to own anything.

Auken's tale also reveals dark, dystopian aspects of life in this future world: Living inside the city, one contends with the looming fear of being punished for one's thoughts and dreams —which are continuously recorded, complete absence of privacy, and mandatory registration for any type of travel. The story also clarifies that the green areas between the cities dare not be touched by citizens; that there are plenty enough trees and grass planted inside the city for people to get a sense of nature there. Outside the city dwell the disaffected, the technologically overwhelmed, and the politically uncompliant, who must fend for themselves in primitive settlements.

Nonetheless, this is the narrative that the WEF offers up to justify our eventual ownership of nothing: A world where the boon of green energy renders personal possessions obsolete and our lives materially carefree, but which —it is unapologetically implied— will be only for those of us willing to give up our unrestricted freedom of movement and our privacy to the point that even our innermost thoughts are no longer our own.

Auken concludes her story by brushing off the annulments of basic human rights as only minor annoyances in what is "All in all...a good life" and expresses that her pity is *really for* "...all the people who do not live in our city. Those we *lost* on the way". Apparently, we are being warned of the consequences of not going along with the plan.

The WEF and the UN tend to use some peculiar catchwords and phrases in the literature of their intertwined agendas that alert us to their influence over a wide range of institutions. If, when reading a corporation's mission statement or a university's code of ethics these days, you encounter the words "equity", "stakeholder", "sustainability" or "reimagine", you can be fairly sure that they are on board the same globalist agenda train headed for the New World Order with an ETA of 2030.

"Equity" is a tricky word. To paraphrase what one recent commentator astutely observed:

> *"Until just a few years ago, the word 'equity' was rarely ever seen outside the pages of an investment prospectus or real-estate contract...but now, it's everywhere".*

Everywhere, indeed. Nowadays, the term "equity" is more readily assumed to be in reference to *social justice*, and it is coming to be perceived as an ideal that the sum total of wealth of the members of a defined group should be apportioned equally among those members without regard for how much of that wealth any particular member is actually entitled to. It seems to me that this word has surreptitiously crept in and replaced "equality" in so many texts that we hardly even noticed. The WEF states that "wealth [is] abundant, thanks to capitalism, but now that wealth needs to be evenly distributed, as socialists have long called for".[75]

Now, the common interpretation of "stakeholder capitalism" is a system in which profit-making enterprises seek not only to enrich their shareholders but also to act responsibly in consideration of the needs of all who may be affected by their business activities. But, what is a stakeholder, really?

It is someone who holds a figurative stake, which —ever since the phrase originated with reference to wooden stakes that marked the claimed boundaries of one's land— means a claim of ownership to something. The WEF advocates an equitable redistribution of wealth and a new system of "stakeholder capitalism",[76] while its expressed view is that we will own nothing by the year 2030.

So, that poses a conundrum: How could anyone possess an equitable share of the society's wealth while simultaneously owning nothing?

I assert that one couldn't... unless the sum of the society's wealth were zero, in which case one's share of it would also be. Zero is nothing, after all. Moreover, how would an economic system of stakeholder capitalism even be possible, if no one actually had a stake of ownership in anything (much less, the means of production) or even the ability to accrue profits?

Well, recall that they said *we* would own nothing, but they never said *they* would own nothing. I suspect that after some amount of doubletalk, semantic gymnastics, and legislative sleight of hand, the reality of "stakeholder capitalism" will eventually turn out to be a mixture of capitalism for the stakeholders and socialism for the rest of us.

It seems unlikely that Ida Auken's tale of green energy displacing fossil fuels to the effect of causing everything to become free will actually come true by 2030, if ever.

So, "How would they go about redistributing our wealth to the point that we would own nothing by 2030?", you might ask. Based on what we've seen thus far, one answer that seems to fit well overall is "establishment of a crisis", or, to be increasingly specific: "crisis mitigation measures", or "financial destruction caused by crisis mitigation measures", or "advantage-taking of the financial destruction caused by crisis mitigation measures".

All of these events constitute "how", because they are parts of a singular process. These are examples of it during the past couple of years:

- Investment firms like Blackrock (whose executive ranks have included at least four of the WEF's Young Global Leaders since 2016) have been buying up single-family homes at rapid pace across the United States[77] from homeowners who are selling to relocate either for new work opportunities in the wake of business closures and job losses resulting from pandemic lockdowns and vaccination mandates or to escape undesirable living conditions in areas where crime rates have risen due to the defunding of police departments to appease Critical Race Theory ideologues.[78] Unfortunately, many of these sellers are discovering after moving out that — due to overbidding by such investment firms which are eager to pick up as many houses as possible at whatever cost,[79] which has artificially skewed home values upward—[80] buying a next house to move into has become impossibly unaffordable.

■ Eviction moratoriums effected by the CDC and US Congress —which they justified firstly to minimize viral transmission and secondly to ease the burden of renters in the prevailing wave of economic hardship resulting from business closures and job losses caused by pandemic lockdowns—[81] [82] have made countless owners of rental properties unable to eject millions of delinquent tenants[83] [84] and replace them with paying ones, thereby putting those property owners at risk of not having the cash flow to keep up with their property loan payments and thus defaulting and having their properties seized by the banks.

■ More directly, many lose their sources of income —again, due to failed businesses and lost jobs caused by pandemic lockdowns and vaccination mandates— and are forced to deplete their savings and liquidate whatever assets they can until eventually running out of money, defaulting on their mortgages and having their homes repossessed.[85]

■ At various points over the years, with the expressed aim of boosting economic growth to address crises of lagging national economies, central banks have enacted fiscal stimulus measures which have increased the available supply of money and credit.[86] [87] Although this may sound good, this is deliberate inflation that equates to a loss in value —relative to other nations' currencies— of the currency in which a nation's citizens get paid and hold their savings. The more that such a nation's economy relies on foreign supplies of goods and services, the more this inflation averages out to an overall increase in the prices for goods and services that one must pay domestically as well, or, to look at it the other way around, a decrease in the total value of one's money.

Obviously, the above process of depleting the wealth of the populace is a loosely-controlled one whose effects are realized only gradually over time. However, the powers that be may be creeping toward a new, more direct strategy that would be able to kill two proverbial birds with one stone:

■ The September 2021 Biden-nominee for the U.S. Comptroller of the Currency, Saule Omarova, who was born and raised in Soviet-era Kazakhstan and wrote her thesis at Moscow State University on Karl Marx's Economic Analysis and the Theory of Revolution in The Capital[88] (although she has denied being a communist[89]), published a controversial paper in the Vanderbilt Law Review entitled, "The People's Ledger: How to Democratize Money and Finance the Economy", wherein she proposed the *obsoletion of private banks* in favor of citizens having current accounts directly with the Federal Reserve instead which would be denominated in a digital currency.

In such a system, naturally, every transaction would be recorded by the Fed. On top of this, Omarova proposed a new fiscal stimulus plan whereby the government could decide to deposit *or withdraw* funds to or from citizens' digital accounts.[90] [91] After having been criticized by both republicans and moderate democrats for her proposed views which they deemed to be socialist and anti-democratic, and while she said that she had not intended to implement the policies described in her paper in her position as the Comptroller, Omarova withdrew her nomination for the Comptroller position. In reaction, U.S. President Biden declared that Omarova had been subjected to inappropriate personal attacks and that he would be looking for another nominee for the position.[92]

✳✳✳

As already pointed out, followers of a Luciferian esoteric philosophy have been striving for decades to shape the spiritual worldview of the United Nations, and the WEF has taken on the task of carrying out the UN's agenda.

The trajectories of these organizations — particularly the trend toward unified global governance and the plan for transhumanism, which will neatly fulfill the visions of Illuminist Adam Weishaupt and occultist Alice Bailey of a New World Order with a new world religion and Bailey's forecast of new forms of human life to be birthed by science—demonstrate that this influence is in effect.

It is, then, no wonder that the UN and WEF are advocating socialism (the underlying Satanic spirit of which I will explain further ahead in my discussion of Marx) and that there has been such a dramatic upsurge over the last two years of acutely leftist, democratic-socialist (or vice versa, as you like), communist-leaning and authoritarian rhetoric and dictates from world leaders and other powerful entities who collaborate with the WEF.

As for religious leaders, many Catholics and other Christians have watched with disbelief lately as the Papacy has been promoting interfaith ecumenism so heavily that it might be interpreted as an advance toward the unification of world religions[93] while equating religious fundamentalism (presumably including even strict adherence to *Catholic* precepts) with "sickness"[94] and, yet, still adamantly adhering to the age-old dictum that spiritual salvation can be attained by Christians *only through* the Roman Catholic church.[95]

All fairly recently, the Pope has proposed an increased level of authority for the United Nations over transnational affairs and obeisance to it,[96] opposed the excommunication of Catholic politicians who support abortion,[97] expressed support for the concept of legal civil unions for same-sex couples[98] and urged followers to accept the new experimental vaccines by proclaiming that receiving a vaccination is "an act of love".[99]

To be sure, as so many world leaders have aligned their policies with the aims of the WEF and the UN, under the slogan of the "Great Reset" (a.k.a. "Build Back Better"), the general public is being shocked by their blatant encouragement of ideas contrary to traditional concepts of morality and religion, such as...

- education of schoolchildren in transgenderism;[100]

- promotion of socially-divisive movements grounded in Marxist class-struggle ideology, such as Critical Race Theory[101] and the victimology of "Wokeness";[102]

- endorsement of lawlessness and societal decay by decriminalizing crimes like burglary[103] and illicit drug use[104] and handicapping law enforcement in high-crime locales by defunding[105] and imposing vaccination mandates on police departments;[106][107]

- financially incentivizing, rather than remedying, joblessness and vagrancy;[108][109][110]

- suspending the property rights of property owners and landowners while encouraging delinquency, trespassing, and squatting;[111][112][113][114]

- cutting off critical transnational fuel supply lines;[115][116][117]

- welcoming and covertly resettling hundreds of thousands of unvetted illegal immigrants into society[118][119] while trying to block legislation requiring that citizens properly identify themselves when voting;[120][121][122]

- declaring unconstitutional vaccination mandates on large employers[123] and even the populations of entire countries;[124][125]

- subjecting citizens to extended lockdowns and travel restrictions;[126][127][128]

- censoring any views contradicting their expressed narratives as "misinformation";[129] [130]

- denying citizens' rights of assembly and freedom of expression by disrupting legal, peaceful public protests;[131] [132] [133]

- arming an infamous terrorist group in the Middle East with tens of billions of dollars' worth of advanced military weapons and vehicles[134] while abandoning a substantial number of free-world citizens and their supporters behind that enemy's lines to be hunted down and made examples of.[135] [136]

As long as the power of these actors remains unchecked, the list of offenses will undoubtedly go on.

"If I didn't know better, this administration, I would actually believe, is almost purposely trying to destroy the United States of America. I've never seen anything like it."

—Congressman Jeff Van Drew, September 21, 2021[137]

I assert that these are all tactics of a strategy of demoralization of society —a planned process of devolution meant to manifest a sort of *hell on earth*— as part of a broader objective of ideological subversion of the kind that we were warned about for years by ex-Soviet KGB operatives, which I will discuss further on.

After all, in doing any *re*-set, or to build anything *back* better, an original structure must be destroyed. In this strategy, we can recognize an operative principle that could be called *Ordo ab chao* (order out of chaos) which is, according to *An Encyclopædia of*

Freemasonry and its Kindred Sciences, a motto of the 33rd degree;[137B] that is, the highest attainable rank in (Scottish Rite) Freemasonry[137C] and, according to some, also the level by which a mason has doubtless been made aware of the secret identity of the *god of the Lodge*.[137D]

Satanism, Communism and Witchcraft

Could this accelerating outbreak of veiled Luciferian activity, being spread around the globe through the agendas of these preeminent organizations and world leaders, also be emboldening more overt Satanic factions?

Organized Satanism has recently been rearing its head more proudly than before, perhaps taking its cue from the emerging globalist wave of the sinister.

In 2020, the independent group, Satanic Delco, made the news in an article in the Philadelphia Inquirer, intended, no doubt, to warm the hearts of readers, about its charitable "To Hell with Homelessness" campaign.[138]

In 2021, the Satanic Temple of Dallas, Fort Worth and Houston filed a lawsuit against the State of Texas challenging new regulations that prohibit abortion once a baby's heartbeat is detected, arguing that it infringed on their religious liberty by preventing them from exploiting late-term abortions as ritual child sacrifices.[139]

Also in 2021, the Satanic Temple installed a sculpture at the Illinois State Capitol depicting Baphomet (the Capricorn personification of Satan) as an infant as a gesture of opposition to the presence of baby Jesus in the nativity scene display there.[140]

In 2022, an After School Satan Club commenced meetings at a primary school in Moline, Illinois[141] and another in Lebanon, Ohio.[142] The Satanic Temple admitted that it intends to hold After School Satan Club meetings *only* at schools which host Good News Club meetings, for the explicit purpose of opposing that club's Christian influence.

***

Although it will shock many to learn, there is abundant evidence that Karl Marx —in spite of his promotion of atheism via communism which, he asserted, superseded and would bring about the disappearance of, existing religions—[143] was a devotee of the devil.

Marx's affinity for Satan and his sympathetic desire to degrade, subdue and annihilate the human race is evident in his personal writings, the attestations to his personal character given by close friends and associates and his correspondence with them, as well as the declared aims and consequences of communist rule for societies throughout history.

> *"Worlds I would destroy forever, Since I can create no world"*

> *"I shall build my throne high overhead, Cold, tremendous shall its summit be. For its bulwark — superstitious dread, For its marshal —blackest agony."*

> *"See this sword? The prince of darkness sold it to me."*

"With Satan I have struck my deal, He chalks the signs, beats time for me. I play the death march fast and free."

The lines above are excerpted from various poems and plays written by Karl Marx,[144] [145] the self-proclaimed "Pope of Communism".[146]

Marx's hate of humanity and rejection of God's authority mirrored the sentiments of Satan, as documented in the Abrahamic scriptures. In the 1986 book, *Marx & Satan*, by an Evangelical Lutheran priest named Richard Wurmbrand who had endured years of imprisonment and horrific torture in communist Romania for the crime of preaching Christianity, to settle any doubt that these may simply have been the offhanded musings of a young man during a fleeting moment of emotional darkness that he later grew out of, Wurmbrand presented compelling evidence that Marx did hold on to his obsession with Satan and murderous urges long after he wrote those lines in his early twenties.

Marx was born into a Jewish family and was raised as a Christian who, by all accounts, was rather devout in his beliefs until —suddenly and inexplicably— he turned *anti-theist*. That is to say that he still believed in the existence of, but rejected, God.[147] Preaching atheism to his disciples would have been both his secret slight against God and, of course, a means of dispelling the notion of any higher authority for a man to obey than the communist party.

Although the spirit of communism may superficially appear to be humanitarian, championing the cause of equity for the poorer classes, the body of evidence depicting Marx's character makes that hard to swallow. It is much easier to grasp how his focus on raising the social station of the less fortunate was 1) to win over the hearts and minds of the majority (which happens to be the lower economic class in virtually every society) and polarize society at its two economic extremes to create more of a perceived gulf between them and 2) to stoke the flames of resentment high enough to compel working class citizens to rally in government-sanctioned campaigns of mass violence and murder against minority bourgeoisie citizens that they believe are the root of their problems. Assuming that Marx did understand human nature as well as he professed, that was what he intended by "class struggle", as evidenced by the blood-stained pages of Soviet and Communist Chinese history.[148]

Moreover, the same basic strategy was employed to carry out the holocaust in Nazi Germany, targeting the Jews as the scapegoated class.[149] Although this is not attributed to *communism, per se*, it was still perpetrated under the banner of *Nationalsozialismus* (National *Socialism*).

Having said that, I digress for a moment to reflect on a question that might arise in the minds of some: "Even as we sit here now, attempting to piece together a puzzle illustrating an organized scheme of wealthy elitists meant to deprive the rest of us of our possessions and human rights, are we not blindly succumbing to the same Bourgeoisie-hating mindset that Marxism encourages?"

In answer to that, I point out that Marxism seeks to vilify the privileged class regardless of any operative reality. Just how sound our conclusions are about the current situation depends on whether we arrive at them more through prejudices about wealthy people, generally, having nefarious intentions or through facts and evidence indicating that some of them, specifically, do.

I believe that the goal of leveling out the socioeconomic position of all is counter to human nature: It is the God-given instinct for survival and progression of the species that compels man and animal alike to seek to improve its circumstances. It is unrealistic to expect that a status quo where everyone in a society has equal wealth can be maintained naturally after having been brought about by artificial forces. Whatever motivations people may have to strive for more than they have, whether the simple fulfillment of basic needs, the sense of entitlement to be compensated for one's labor according to one's ability, or insatiable greed, there will inevitably be those who end up with more or less than others, and discernible socioeconomic strata will prevail.

Although the human instinct to attain or achieve devolves into greed if unrestrained, the instinct is not innately wrong. However, Marx's philosophy effectively criminalizes the human urge to accumulate. By the logic of this ideology, anyone who manages to attain a degree of material success greater than another does risks being labeled as an oppressor and eliminated for it.

Marxist ideology encourages the continual rebellion of society against itself, through a repetitive process of culling which eventually results in societal self-destruction. In this system, each revolution (which we should interpret here as "cycle", so as to avoid any romantic idealism and focus on its mechanistic nature) targets for elimination the members of the perceived class of oppressors in the society and redistributes their wealth among the masses, thereby yielding a newly equitized population.

Then, after some amount of time, due to man's natural accumulative urge and the ability of some to find ways of amassing more wealth than others, the society once again comes to view itself as economically stratified and therefore oppressed by the next uppermost stratum which it rationalizes must then also be purged. After churning through enough of these cycles, this Satanic meat grinder eventually achieves its logical conclusion: The destruction of a society by its own hands and, for the majority's having unrepentantly committed those murders out of envy and vengeance against the minority, the damnation of their souls and, thus, victory for Satan.

The working of witchcraft does not necessarily resemble what we have been popularly conditioned to recognize as magic. I believe that more powerful forms of witchcraft are being wrought in today's world by practitioners in business suits and white laboratory coats than by those in any traditional witches' garb. As was explained by the late Pastor Derek Prince, the essence of witchcraft is a spirit of *rebellion against God*, and its presence is simply discerned as *the use of manipulation and/or intimidation to achieve domination.*[150] It is, in effect, the *use of unholy spirits to bend reality to one's will.*

Marxism leverages a spirit of manipulation of vulnerability in a society in order to establish its position of power and a spirit of intimidation to maintain its domination and, by these criteria, is a large-scale form of witchcraft. Despite the outward absence of esoteric rituals or anything spiritual in Marxist doctrine, one may ponder whether the one-hundred million deaths of unarmed civilians that have resulted from the actions or negligence of Marxist regimes throughout history —also known as the infamous "Communist Death Toll"—[151] may have actually served the purpose of Satanic ritual human sacrifice. One should not assume that all communists are actually atheists who are oblivious to the final destination of the path they walk.

The apocryphal *Book of Enoch*, which, although shrouded in mystery as to its authorship and controversy among Jewish and Christian theologians as to its legitimacy as part of the biblical canon (with the exceptions of Beta Israel and the Orthodox Church in Ethiopia and the Orthodox Tewahedo Church in Eritrea[152]), nonetheless relates a story that is interesting to consider:

Its component *Book of the Watchers* tells of the time when two hundred fallen angels descended to earth, mated with human women to produce their hybrid offspring (who were the same Nephilim described in *Genesis*[153]) and revealed "the eternal secrets which were preserved in heaven, which men were striving to learn" (1 Enoch 9:6), including those mentioned in the *Old Testament* as having been expressly forbidden by God such as enchantments and astrology,[154] as well as other arts and sciences that we might interpret in modern terms as the hybridization of plants, chemistry, astronomy, geology and meteorology, bestowing upon humans a sense of having supernatural powers.

The Watchers also taught the making of metal weapons and armor, which emboldened men to be more warlike and lethal in battle. They taught the making of various types of jewelry, adornments and cosmetics for women to artificially beautify themselves, which made them more sexually alluring to men. By revealing such occult and scientific bodies of knowledge, the fallen angels stimulated mankind's sinful urges; the thirst for spiritual and physical power, pride, greed, vanity and lust; and amplified the havoc caused thereby.[155]

This story in *Enoch*, which recounts the fall of mankind yet another rung further from divine grace after the incident in Eden, as a consequence of once more having succumbed to Satan's enticement with secret knowledge, illustrates Satan's pattern of using *information* —and particularly that which we are not qualified to possess— as a means of inducing humanity's self-destruction.

Is it any wonder that, of all of mankind's technological advancements, the one having the greatest overall potential is the one with the potential to annihilate us all in an instant?

"Now I am become death, the destroyer of worlds."

—J. Robert Oppenheimer

(recalling a passage from the *Bhagavad Gita,* in reflection, after having witnessed the explosion of the first atomic bomb[156])

This helps us to understand why any system of belief which *embodies the occult,* or which *embraces science and rejects God,* is not merely pagan or atheistic but is also therefore inherently Satanic.

So frequently today, we find the word "narrative" being used to describe someone's expressed view of reality. Actually, a narrative is simply a story that someone is telling, irrespective of what is true or real. Since when did people begin defining existence and purpose in terms of narratives rather than reality? The implication seems to be that we can choose to play a character role in whichever story of reality we accept.

Consider the word "re*imagine*" —a favorite in the vocabulary of globalists like Klaus Schwab who intend to radically transform the world in such a way as to prime its population for total draconian domination— and what it suggests about their perception of reality. It suggests that the present reality is merely an illusion that can be altered by *imagi*nation. In Edith Kermit Roosevelt's article which was mentioned earlier, she also provided a salient quotation from the prominent 19th-century occultist and founder of the Theosophical Society, Helena Blavatsky, concerning the influence of *magic* on history:

> *"What is one to do, when in order to rule men, it is necessary to deceive them? ... For almost invariably the more simple, the more silly, and the more gross the phenomenon, the more likely is it to succeed."* [157]

Now, consider the warning against the above in the following statement:

> *"Ideological subversion ... is to change the perception of reality ... to such an extent that —despite the abundance of information— no one is able to come to sensible conclusions in the interest of defending themselves, their families, their community and their country"*

> —Yuri Alexandrovich Bezmenov[158]

Yuri Bezmenov was a covert operative for the Soviet KGB during the Cold War era. During his career, he was stationed in India, firstly as an undercover propagandist working as a journalist for the state-run RIA Novosti news service and, later, in another position gathering intelligence from spies and influential Indian citizens.[159] After having discovered that an Indian friend of his was on a list of individuals who were targeted for elimination by the communist regime, he decided to defect and managed his escape to Canada in 1970.

In 1984, initially under the pseudonym of Tomas Schuman, he began issuing public warnings wherein he revealed the long-term, four-stage strategy of "active measures" (i.e. psychological warfare) that the Soviets routinely employed in the ideological subversion of enemy nations. He emphasized that the primary objective of this activity is to destroy the nation of the enemy and that, ironically, the majority of what it entails is "overt, legitimate and easily observable".

Many of the events that Bezmenov described are eerily similar to those that are visibly happening in the United States and around the world today, even to the extent that various aspects of what he outlined as distinct and sequential stages of demoralization, destabilization and crisis seem to be occurring at different degrees simultaneously:

Stage 1: Demoralization (over a period of 15-20 years)

> *Brainwashing of a single generation with Marxist-Leninist ideology.* Bezmenov said, in a filmed interview with G. Edward Griffin in 1984, that the process of demoralization had already been completed even beyond the original expectations of the Soviet leadership. He explained that, by the time demoralization is complete, the society is no longer able to clearly distinguish true from false or right from wrong.

Target Areas:

<u>Religion</u>   *Destroy*, ridicule, replace respected organizations with fake ones; distract attention from the real faith and direct it toward various different faiths.

<u>Education</u>   *Distract* from learning of constructive, pragmatic and efficient subjects.

<u>Social</u>   *Remove* individuals' sense of social initiative, responsibility and naturally-established links within society and delegate them to artificial, bureaucratically-controlled bodies, e.g. social workers who are not personally interested.

<u>Power Structure</u>   *Eclipse* the authority of traditionally-elected (or thereby appointed) administrative bodies by the influential power of non-elected bodies, such as media outlets.

<u>Labor Relations</u>   *Interfere*, through labor unions, in the natural process of negotiation between employee and employer, thereby depriving the worker of the right to determine a personally acceptable minimum wage for work; encourage workers' strikes to incite violence, destruction of property and disruptions in the supply of critical goods and services.

<u>Law & Order</u>   *Vilify* legitimate police and military efforts and empathize with criminal behaviors; portray criminals as

products of their environment and victims of an inhumane legal system.

Stage 2: **Destabilization** (over a period of 2-5 years)

Disruption of all relationships, accepted institutions and organizations in the country of the enemy. The numerous, opposing points of view resulting from the demoralization of the society lead to conflicts where no common ground can be found as a starting point for peaceful resolution. Radical and extreme measures are taken in economics, legislation, law enforcement, and the media, leading to intense confrontations. Embedded "sleeper" agents become especially active within their spheres of influence in society to facilitate these disruptions.

Stage 3: **Crisis** (over a period of 2-6 months)

Society can no longer function productively and collapses. Despair prevails. The population is looking for a savior. Religious groups are hoping for a messiah to come. Workers are concerned about feeding their families. Citizens begin thinking that a stronger, perhaps centralized, government is needed. Non-elected committees (harboring Marxist-Leninist interests), appear and offer unconventional solutions. At this stage, the society is subjected to either 1) civil war or 2) invasion, which is followed by Normalization.

Stage 4: **Normalization** (to last for an indefinite period)

The self-appointed new rulers bring stability to the nation by force. Radical and revolutionary-minded actors who have fulfilled their function in bringing about destabilization, including sleeper agents, liberal activists, social workers, academics and homosexuals, Bezmenov said, are no longer tolerated and summarily exterminated. Bezmenov explained that this is simply because the psychological shock — when they see what the *beautiful society of equality and social justice* actually means in practice— will cause them to revolt.

Bezmenov posited that, by the time Normalization occurs, the process of subversion can be reversed only through military intervention, whereas, it can still be reversed at the Crisis stage by supporting the right-wing conservative cause.[160] [161]

Crisis Diplomacy, Propaganda & Lies

How can one destroy a society's economy with the consent and cooperation of the society itself?

Identify a crisis (or fabricate one); ideally, one that can be blamed on an invisible enemy whose threat-level is difficult to ascertain and whose existence, even, is hard to disprove. Persuade the public to unite against this common enemy, inundate them with messages that provoke such a level of fear that their ability to think critically is impaired, and convince them that —in the best interest of all— they must urgently comply with the officially-prescribed defensive measures and make any personal sacrifices necessary to resolve the crisis. Maintain the public perception that the crisis is ongoing until the objective has been achieved. Does this sound familiar today?

As an example, cite climate change as an imminent existential threat to humanity. Insist that the public's own use of fossil fuels is to blame for it, and demand that they stop using them, thereby destroying economies that rely on them for their economic survival.

As another example, engineer a pandemic using a virus that is non-lethal to most people but characterize it as an existential threat to humanity, exaggerate the public's fear by paying hospitals incentives to label deaths as virus-caused and changing the rules so that the virus is invariably listed as the primary cause of death on death certificates whenever the deceased were found to have been infected, manipulate statistics of hospitalizations resulting from a well-known seasonal virus that causes similar symptoms to make them appear to be due to the new virus, insist that extended lockdowns, repeated vaccinations and the gradual relinquishment of personal freedoms are necessary to resolve the situation, and observe as these measures cause widespread business disruptions, debt defaults, foreclosures, joblessness and homelessness.

There is ample evidence suggesting that both of the above scenarios have been orchestrated.

As for evidence of the crisis surrounding climate change having been engineered, let us begin by looking at the think tank called the Club of Rome (COR) which was co-founded by David Rockefeller in 1968[162] as a catalyst for change through the identification and analysis of the crucial problems facing humanity.

In 1991, the COR published a report entitled *The First Global Revolution* which outlined a strategy to transition nation states into a system of world governance, by focusing on economy, technology, mass media, food control, water availability, environment, energy, pollution growth, religion and education.

In this report, the COR unabashedly admitted that *it was its own idea* to leverage a perceptual threat of man-made environmental crisis to compel the world population to unitedly yield to increased governmental control in order to resolve it. In the report, it said:

> "*The need for enemies seems to be a common historical factor. The ploy of finding a scapegoat is as old as mankind itself. Bring the divided nation together to face an outside enemy: either a real one, or else one invented for the purpose. Every state has been so used to classifying its neighbors as friend or foe that the sudden absence of traditional adversaries has left governments and public opinion with a great void to fill. New enemies have to be identified, new strategies imagined, new weapons devised.[...] In searching for a new enemy to unite us, <u>we came up with the idea</u> that pollution, the threat of global warming, water shortage, famine and the like would fit the bill.[...] All these dangers are caused by human intervention and it is only through changed attitudes and behavior that they can be overcome. [...] The real enemy, then, is humanity itself.*[emphasis added]"[163]

Also note that, at its third annual conference in 1973, the World Economic Forum (then known as the European Management Symposium) had hosted COR co-founder, Aurelio Peccei, to give a speech to its members discussing his 1972 book entitled *Limits to Growth* which outlined a number of crises including environmental pollution and natural disasters.[164] So, it can be surmised that the COR had established relations with and *transmitted its legacy to the WEF* no later than that.

There have been many political figures since then who have made statements strongly suggesting that climate change has merely been a ruse to garner public support to facilitate globalist objectives. One of the most noteworthy, as he was a member of the Club of Rome apparently until his death in 2022, was Mikhail Gorbachev, the final leader of the Soviet

Union, who said in 1996, "The threat of environmental crisis will be the international disaster key to unlock the New World Order."[165]

Here are several more examples:

"A global warming treaty [Kyoto] must be implemented even if there is no scientific evidence to back the [enhanced] greenhouse effect."

—Richard Benedick,
Deputy Assistant of State[166]

"No matter if the science of global warming is all phony...climate change [provides] the greatest opportunity to bring about justice and equality in the world."

—Christine Stewart,
Former Canadian Minister of the
Environment[167]

"We have got to ride the global warming issue. Even if the theory of global warming is wrong, we will be doing the right thing in terms of economic policy and environmental policy."

—Timothy Wirth, Former U.S. Senator;
President of the UN Foundation[168]

"We may get to the point where the only way of saving the world will be for industrialized civilization to collapse."

—Maurice Strong,
Organizer of the first UN Earth Climate
Summit[169]

Now, confronting the purported threat of climate change is at the forefront of the UN's and WEF's agendas,[170] [171] [172] [173] [174] which adhere to the same idea originally proposed by the Club of Rome (that the enemy is humanity itself) and call for the urgent reduction of carbon emissions to "net zero".[175] Effectively, this translates to the cessation of the burning of fossil fuels. Given that 84% of primary energy comes from fossil fuels, globally,[176] what toll do you suppose this strategy will take on economies that depend on coal, oil and gas for their survival?

Mainly as a consequence of environmental-crisis mentality, the concept of "sustainability" has become ubiquitous in the literature of corporations and universities. The definition of it given by Sustainability UCLA is simple and straightforward:

> *"Sustainability is the balance between the environment, equity and economy"*[177]

By the way, isn't it interesting to see "equity" inserted there? Although this definition may sound righteous and fair enough to spur people to action to set things right, it is no more sensical than "the balance between the growth rate of forests, your life savings and the market price of copper": This purported "balance" is abstract and immeasurable. The claim of those who push this concept (and we're presumably just supposed to take their word for it as long as they keep saying it's true) is that an imbalance exists due to the economy's being prioritized over both the environment and equity, and, so, the solution to bring about equilibrium is bettering the states of the environment and equity and worsening the state of the economy.

Not that protecting the natural environment from needless degradation is an unworthy cause, but the above notion of sustainability just happens to be ideal for persuading people —in the interest of the common good— to jump on the bandwagon to economic suicide while consenting to the leveling of their wealth and (if we take our hints from the WEF's predictions and Ida Auken's tale of 2030) the preening of nature for the exclusive benefit of a group of "stakeholders" who will be entitled to enjoy it.

As for evidence of the pandemic having been orchestrated, let us begin by examining a report published by the Rockefeller Foundation in May 2010 entitled *Scenarios for the Future of Technology and International Development*. The report is presented as an "exercise in scenario planning". It describes a handful of potential future scenarios. The first, starting on page 18, is called "Lockstep: A world of tighter top-down government control and more authoritarian leadership, with limited innovation and growing citizen pushback".[178] The scenario begins this way:

> *"In 2012, the pandemic that the world had been anticipating for years finally hit. Unlike 2009's H1N1, this new influenza strain —originating from wild geese— was extremely virulent and deadly. Even the most pandemic-prepared nations were quickly overwhelmed when the virus streaked around the world, infecting nearly 20 percent of the global population and killing 8 million in just seven months, the majority of them healthy young adults. The pandemic also had a deadly effect on economies: international mobility of both people and goods screeched to a halt, debilitating industries like tourism and breaking global supply chains. Even locally, normally bustling shops and office buildings sat empty for months, devoid of both employees and customers."*

After some parts which I have skipped here, it goes on:

> *"The Chinese government's quick imposition and enforcement of mandatory quarantine for all citizens, as well as its instant and near-hermetic sealing off*

of all borders, saved millions of lives, stopping the spread of the virus far earlier than in other countries and enabling a swifter post pandemic recovery. China's government was not the only one that took extreme measures to protect its citizens from risk and exposure. During the pandemic, national leaders around the world flexed their authority and imposed airtight rules and restrictions, from the mandatory wearing of face masks to body-temperature checks at the entries to communal spaces like train stations and supermarkets. Even after the pandemic faded, this more authoritarian control and oversight of citizens and their activities stuck and even intensified. In order to protect themselves from the spread of increasingly global problems – from pandemics and transnational terrorism to environmental crises and rising poverty – leaders around the world took a firmer grip on power. At first, the notion of a more controlled world gained wide acceptance and approval. Citizens willingly gave up some of their sovereignty – and their privacy – to more paternalistic states in exchange for greater safety and stability."

The whole thing is a revealing read. Except for the exact timing of it, the similarity between the story of the future that the Rockefellers told here and what has actually transpired since 2019 is uncanny; especially the emphasis on China's involvement and the draconian measures it implemented. The UN's WHO certainly did applaud China's handling of matters in real life,[179] as if to portray it as a role model for other nations to emulate, despite that China did not by any means prevent the spread of the disease to the rest of the world and was probably where the virus originated.[180] I suggest we would be wiser to interpret this as a *declaration of intent* than as a prediction, for reasons that I will elucidate further on.

Beyond just a hypothetical scenario that foretold of this pandemic ten years before it happened, the events we have recently actually witnessed include:

1) Dr. Anthony Fauci declared in his speech at Georgetown University in 2017 —in no uncertain terms— that there *would be* a "surprise outbreak" during the forthcoming Trump presidential administration,[181] and then

2) the WEF, the Bill and Melinda Gates Foundation, and Johns Hopkins Center for Health Security coordinated the pandemic scenario called Event 201 to simulate "the effects of a fictional *coronavirus originating in bats*" in October 2019,[182] [183] and then

3) scarcely two months later, in December 2019, in *Wuhan, China,* the first reported *coronavirus* infections were confirmed,[184] and then

4) shortly thereafter, at the start of 2020, the disease was spread throughout the globe by millions of outbound Chinese travellers during the Asian New Year holiday even as China instated lockdowns and travel bans *within its own borders,*[185] and then

5) after Fauci had been questioned in a senate hearing and vehemently denied that his institute had provided any funding for "gain-of-function" research on *coronaviruses* by the *Chinese Wuhan Institute of Virology (WIV)* from whose labs the novel coronavirus is suspected to have leaked,[186] it was discovered that the NIH had indeed —albeit indirectly, through a non-profit organization named EcoHealth Alliance— provided at least $599,000 *to the WIV for gain-of-function coronavirus experimentation on bats* between 2018-2019,[187] and then

6) the spike protein of the virus was found to contain a genetic sequence that is not known to exist *in any other virus in the world* and yet happens to have been *patented* (US patent 9,587,003) *in 2017 by Moderna, the manufacturer of one of the novel vaccines.*[188]

> *"The changes we have already seen in response to COVID-19 prove that a reset of our economic and social foundations is possible. This is our best chance to instigate stakeholder capitalism ..."*

> —World Economic Forum, June 3, 2020[189]

> *"We have a golden opportunity to seize something good from this crisis — its unprecedented shockwaves may well make people more receptive to big visions of change. As we move from rescue to recovery, we have a unique but rapidly shrinking window of opportunity to learn lessons and reset ourselves on a more sustainable path. It is an opportunity we have never had before and may never have again."*[190]

—HRH Charles, Prince of Wales (joint initiator of the Great Reset Dialogues with the WEF[191]), June 3, 2020

When the WEF announced its launch of the Great Reset, it was quite clearly tied directly to the pandemic:

> *"There is an urgent need for global stakeholders to cooperate in simultaneously managing the direct consequences of the COVID-19 crisis. To improve the state of the world, the World Economic Forum is starting the Great Reset initiative".*[192]

Do not be deceived by the altruistic tone of the announcement: The Great Reset has never been a pandemic rescue plan. It is a plan for the upheaval and radical restructuring of existing sovereign systems of economy and governance which was initiated at the precise moment to take advantage of weaknesses during a crisis. When the WEF called on "stakeholders to cooperate", you can be sure it was speaking to the ultra-wealthy and influential elites in its Davos Group,[193] not to you or me.

It is very plain to see, from the WEF's own statements and those of its cohorts, that they have stood to gain from the pandemic and its resulting fallout to facilitate its agenda to amass global wealth and control. It did have a motive to bring about the pandemic. Does it seem like more than an unrelated coincidence that the WEF was a key organizer of the pandemic simulation shortly before the breakout occurred?

> *"A lie you tell once remains a lie. A lie you tell a thousand times becomes truth"*[194]

> —Joseph Goebbels,
> German Reich Minister of Propaganda (1933-1945)[195]

In broken-record-player fashion, governments around the world have incessantly repeated, like a mantra, that the novel vaccines are "safe and effective" and nearly all major media outlets have dutifully parroted that phrase to the public. Simply saying something repeatedly does not make it true, although it does have the effect of convincing many that it is when coming from the mouths of supposedly trustworthy people. This is the nature of propaganda.

I daresay that, if you had asked almost anyone in 2018 whether, in order to avoid contracting a virus similar to the common flu, they would be willing to be injected with an experimental drug containing a gene-therapy agent that had never been tested on humans before, the answer would have been "No, never".

Nevertheless, what could be called a cult of "*Inoculism*" has swept through the world, led by its high priest Dr. Fauci. Its followers submit unquestioningly to his authority and follow – on blind faith – the rituals prescribed in his doctrine of "The Science". Donning masks in symbolic sacrifice of their individualities in deference to the Master, they are baptized in the holy fluid of *pharmakeia*. At heretics who choose to remain unsanctified, they glare and spit the accusation through clenched teeth, "Antivax!"

> *"He will use every kind of evil deception to fool those on their way to destruction, because they refuse to love and accept the truth that would save them. For this reason God sends them a powerful delusion so that they will believe the lie."*
>
> —2 Thessalonians 2:10 (NLT), 2:11 (NIV)

The "safe and effective" claim is obviously not credible when viewed in the light of common sense and a bit of common knowledge.

In addition to the well-established fact that *vaccinated individuals can still catch and spread the virus*,[196] which flies in the face of the world public's long-held understanding of the very *meaning and purpose of a vaccine*, statistical data show the effectiveness of these vaccines to be negligible in preventing infection.

Before we begin to delve into some statistics, though, it is important to recognize that in populations where the vaccinated comprise the vast majority, and the vaccines are known to be unreliable, probability alone suggests that the sheer number of vaccinated people who are infected may be higher than the number of unvaccinated who are infected. So, this is an unreliable measure of vaccine effectiveness.

What is more meaningful is the *percentage* of the vaccinated group that is infected compared with the *percentage* of the unvaccinated group that is infected. If we take, as an example, the data from the State Serum Institute of Denmark detailing the vaccination statuses of infected people between November 22nd and December 14th, 2021,[197] considered together with the total population of the country (5,825,743 [198]) and the percentage of its population (77%) that was "fully vaccinated" at the time[199] (which means double-dosed with the vaccines that are issued in this country 200), what we see is that there was barely a difference between the percentage of the fully vaccinated who got infected (1.53%) and the percentage of unvaccinated who got infected (1.67%). [See Appendix A]

If we take for granted —as Big Pharma and our governments would like us to— that these vaccines have the *causative effect* of immunity, then these statistics show that being fully vaccinated was almost totally *ineffective*.

If we analyze a similar set of data from the UK Health Security Agency for the period of February 6th to 27th, 2022,[201] from a slightly different angle by taking into account all vaccinated people, we discover roughly the same outcome. Of the total population in the kingdom (68,468,489 [202]), 77.03% had one or more vaccinations.[203] During the period in question, the infected percentages were 1.61% of the vaccinated and 1.55% of the unvaccinated groups, and so, here again, there was no significant difference. [See Appendix B] Even if we dismiss the idea of causation (as health authorities tend to do when it comes to correlations between vaccinations and adverse events), there is still no correlation between vaccinations and immunity to be seen here either.

Given roughly the same infection rate in the populations of both countries regardless of vaccination status, we might expect *the same amount of protection from wearing shoes.*

Lest we be accused of not looking at enough data, let us also look at the numbers from the UK for the overlapping period of February 13th to March 6th, 2022. [204] Here we see something similar to that above, as well as something more revealing. Of the total population in the kingdom (68,497,716 [205]), 76.8% (as of 2/24; calculated here from the reported number of vaccinated as a percentage of the estimated population[206]) had one or more vaccinations. During the period in question, the infected percentages were 1.35% of the vaccinated and 1.05% of the unvaccinated groups. I will leave it to statisticians and epidemiologists to decide whether this difference is statistically significant, but I do notice that the ratio of vaccinated infected to unvaccinated infected is higher than was shown by the data for the previous time period. Now, here is what else we can see: When we examine the vaccinated population that was infected, and we break this Down into subgroups by the number of vaccine doses received, it becomes apparent that — except in the under-18 age group— there was a *positive correlation* between the number of doses received and the percentage of the infected. There was a *marked increase* in the percentage of infected among those who'd had the second dose, and an even *sharper increase* among those who'd had the third dose. People who had been <u>triple-jabbed comprised a majority (77%) of the infected vaccinated population</u>. [See Appendix C]

Can we assume that this means the *more* vaccinations you get, the *greater* your chances of being infected are? Well, the above data does seem to generally support that. To be sure, it wasn't the infections that caused the vaccinations. However, before we jump to the conclusion that the vaccines caused the infections, we should keep in mind that yacht ownership and wealth are also positively correlated, but neither one "causes" the other, per se; however, being rich is definitely *more conducive to the possibility* of owning a yacht than being poor is. What is certain, though, is that if the vaccines worked to resist infection and became increasingly effective after each added dose then we would expect to see overall divergence on the chart between the number of doses and percentage of infections in the vaccinated population; not convergence as we see here.

Going a step further in looking at the same UK data for February 13th to March 6th, 2022, we see that among the vaccinated who were infected and admitted into overnight hospital emergency care within 28 days of having been diagnosed, there was also an overall positive correlation between the number of doses received and those events. This effect was most pronounced in the 80-or-over age group and decreased gradually over the younger groups but was still positive in all except the under-18 group. <u>People who had received their third shots also comprised a majority (77%) of the infected vaccinated population that was admitted to the ER</u> under these circumstances. [See Appendix D]

This added discovery forces us to add on to the previous question, so that we're now asking whether this all means "The more shots you get, the more likely you are to become infected... *and end up in the emergency room?*" Remember that those pushing the vaccines are aware of the doubts that these data raise, and yet they're still pushing the vaccines.

By the way, when did we lose our grip on the *meaning of vaccination?* Most of us never wonder why we've never encountered the measles, mumps or rubella in our lifetimes or of those of anyone we know, since we received protective injections against them during childhood. So, why is it that more people are not questioning why populations are still becoming infected with this novel virus after having been inoculated against it? I suggest that this is because we have been spoon-fed nonsense, which we have swallowed little by little for long enough that our collective perception of reality has been distorted: We have been transported from the reality where we knew that vaccines were supposed to prevent infection to this new dimension where we accept that they are not meant to.

Ironically, the footnotes in the UK data report mentioned here include this statement:

> *"Comparing case rates among vaccinated and unvaccinated populations should not be used to estimate vaccine effectiveness"*.

Why not? I submit that it is because doing the simple math makes it too apparent that the vaccines are not doing their job. No, they insist, vaccine effectiveness has, rather, been "formally estimated from a number of different sources and is summarized on pages 4 to 15 in this report".[207] I suggest that they want to make what is easy to see look more complicated than it is; hoping that referring us to eleven more pages of factoring for unseen variables, caveats, gray areas, and other exceptions will coax (or exasperate) us into accepting that something which plainly appears not to be working actually is. This is an assault on common sense. I shudder to think about the characters who attend roundtables just to reach consensus on how to best convolute the presentation of data to deceive people.

The lie about safety is even more blatant. It is *impossible* for anyone to say with any certainty that a drug is safe without also knowing its potential side effects over time. The indisputable fact is that *no one knows* what the long-term effects of newly-developed vaccines might be before any long-term human safety trials have been carried out.

Consider that even if every person who had received a vaccine were to become seriously ill or die within a few years, the governments, the public health authorities and the pharmaceutical corporations that have aggressively pushed the vaccination agenda all along would likely hope to stand, blameless, behind the same dictum as they do today: "Correlation does not imply causation".[208] [209]

On the other hand, whenever they credit the vaccines with preventing illness and saving lives, what they are saying is that *correlation is causation.* Although, as a rule, it does require in-depth, scientifically-controlled studies to evidence causation, "the *evidence* generated by most epidemiological studies *is correlational* which, although potentially powerful, <u>cannot be presumed to be causal</u> [emphasis added]";[210] and how reassuring *that* must be for those who would prefer not to acknowledge causation. It seems that they apply this rule *stringently* when it comes to reporting post-vaccination *adverse events* but *loosely* when it comes to claiming *vaccine effectiveness*. If that's not true, then we should be asking how they're progressing with the controlled studies on adverse events that they should be doing based on glaring trends we can all see in the VAERS[211] [212] and Yellow Card[213] reporting systems – to assess whether causality exists or not.

Unless and until results of such controlled studies materialize to actually settle the matter, we can expect the viewpoint of these authorities to remain slanted in the same direction: After receiving the injection, if you do not become infected, then it is assumed that the vaccine protected you, but if you become paralyzed, then it is not assumed that the vaccine was responsible. The reason for the double-standard in the application of logic here is not hard to understand: They say whatever suits their aim, which is to persuade everyone that the vaccinations are harmless and to receive the injections regardless of the consequences.

The infuriating reality is that, while the world wide web is flooded with pages upon pages of statements from so-called "fact checkers" and public health authorities denouncing the "misinterpretation" and "misuse" of vaccine adverse event reports by some to falsely portray the vaccines as dangerous since the reports alone cannot serve as proof before they are investigated, it is also practically barren of statements assuring the concerned public that those reports are actually being investigated.

These near-term events, given their number as well as their severity in many cases, warrant serious investigation and —unless and until the vaccines can be objectively ruled out as the cause— should be cautiously viewed as indicators of potentially serious adverse effects that might develop over the longer term across the overall vaccinated population.

It seems that Big Pharma and the CDC had to be cornered by the undeniable frequency of myocarditis events following vaccinations[214] [215] before they conceded it was actually a side-effect. Could it be that more proactive investigation into these incidents —especially sudden deaths— is not being done by those responsible for public health because health is not the primary aim of these vaccines?

On that note, here is food for thought: By now, it is no secret that Bill Gates, a man who is clearly interested in pandemic scenario modeling and has contributed heavily to the development and proliferation of these novel vaccines[216] (and who also happens to have been one of the WEF's very first Global Leaders for Tomorrow, Class of 1993 [217]), has been accused of being a eugenics proponent. In particular, reports of adverse events from Gates-funded vaccination programs that were carried out in India and Africa have been the bases of allegations of Gate's intent to reduce the growth of indigenous populations by reproductively sterilizing them.[218] [219] Some suspect that Gates is carrying on the tradition of the Rockefeller dynasty (of which he is a descendant[220]) Starting with John D. Rockefeller, Jr. (nicknamed "Junior"), in his zeal for population reduction inspired by his Malthus-leaning professors at Brown University in the late 1890s, the Rockefellers began funding eugenics projects in the early 1900s.[221]

As it so happens, Bill Gates' father – to whom he attributes a fascination from youth with issues of reproduction[222] was on the national board of directors of Planned Parenthood[223]. That organization

Crisis Diplomacy, Propaganda & Lies

arose from the American Birth Control League,[224] which was founded by the notorious eugenicist, Margaret Sanger, and funded with Rockefeller money.[225]

John D. Rockefeller, Jr.

by Unknown Photographer 1920 - From National Photo Company Collection, Public Domain

Sanger was unabashedly outspoken on her view of birth control as a method of weeding out the "unfit" and preventing the birth of "defectives"[226], and she began receiving funding for her Birth Control Research Bureau from Junior Rockefeller in 1924.[227]

Although Sanger is reputed not to have been a racist and did collaborate with African-American community leaders[228], she has been criticized for having turned a blind eye to the racist sentiments of other members of eugenicist circles in which she worked.[229] Moreover, she had a noteworthy member of the Ku Klux Klan, the writer Lothrop Stoddard, as a founding and board member of her American Birth Control League[230] and once made the rather racially-evocative statement that she envisioned the new contraceptive pill would "be used in poverty stricken slums, *jungles* [emphasis added] and among the most ignorant people."[231]

In her writings, Sanger praised the neo-Malthusian movement in Great Britain for its bravery and expressed thanks for its support of her.[232] Bill Gates has also alluded to having once had "sort of a Malthusian view" that the improvement of health conditions of impoverished populations would only exacerbate overpopulation, leading to further scarcity of resources and impoverishment. That was, he clarified, until he came to understand that the decreased likelihood of childhood deaths within healthy populations serves to decrease the perceived need of parents to bear more offspring to offset that risk.

Now, if one *had* harbored any suspicions about Gates' intentions, one might interpret from the above that this epiphany reoriented his thinking about how to manage sustainable population growth: that he would thereafter be inclined toward *improving* the health of a population and not the opposite.

However, before a sigh of relief is warranted, one might also ponder this: If Gates had not arrived at his revised conclusion (which, naturally, was the case until he purportedly did) that health is a solution, rather than a contributing factor, to the problem of overpopulation, then what would his solution have been? It does seem that his position on saving lives *hinges upon the condition* that he thinks doing so would be favorable to the future. Consider this ethos and ask yourself whether you would entrust your life or those of your children to his hands.

Incidentally, it was also Junior Rockefeller who started the Rockefeller Foundation, with which the Bill and Melinda Gates Foundation partnered in 2007 to form the Alliance for a Green Revolution in Africa (AGRA).[233] For further evidence of interconnections among Gates, the Rockefellers, the United Nations and the World Economic Forum, note that Rajiv J. Shah, also a WEF protégé who was inaugurated as a Young Global Leader in 2007 and who is now the President of the Rockefeller Foundation,[234] previously held the various positions of Director for Agricultural Development & Financial Services, Deputy Director for Policy & Finance for Global Health, and Senior Economist at the Bill & Melinda Gates Foundation and was an economist at the UN's World Health Organization.[235]

Besides Rajiv Shah and Gates himself, at least four other executives of the Bill and Melinda Gates Foundation have been either Global Leaders for Tomorrow or Young Global Leaders of the WEF. The Gates' foundation also happens to be one of the most generous private donors to the UN's World Health Organization, having pledged over $682 million dollars to the WHO in support of a vaccination initiative focused on Africa and Asia.[236]

Declarations of Intent

"MAGICK is the Science and Art of causing Change to occur in Conformity with Will"

"Every intentional act is a magical act. [...] By 'intentional' I mean 'willed'"

—Aleister Crowley, *Magick in Theory and Practice*, 1929 [236B]

In the realm of occultism, it is commonly held that outwardly declaring one's intent is crucial in practicing magic. If one performs an online search, one will find innumerable pages containing instructions and advice on invocations and incantations where "declare your intent" is emphasized as a crucial step. Declaration of intent is generally a required step for one's initiation into occult groups as well as a means of amplifying one's power and likelihood of success in performing spells to manifest desired realities.

An occultist's compulsion to openly declare the intent to achieve any nefarious objective is naturally at odds with the need to conceal the fact of that from others. Though the declaration of intent is seen as necessary to magnify one's occult energies to reach the aim, declaring it so overtly as to genuinely alert others to the threat beforehand and allow them a chance to prepare a defense would be contrary to the aim.

The solution is in employing subtlety that allows for intent to be at once both openly admitted and obscured, especially when presented in the midst of a cascade of lies.

> *"Because there is no righteousness in their mouths, but evil is within them, and their throats are like opened tombs and their tongues subvert."*

—Psalms 5:9 (HPBT)

Furthermore, for those who have forewarned of their intent to destroy their prey, the fact that their prey have blissfully ignored the warning and accepted their demise without a struggle is savored as proof of the weakness and stupidity that justified their destruction.

I believe that various participants in this world scheme have openly declared their intent. The UN and the WEF are candidly open about their agendas, announcing them on the internet and at endless meetings of which video recordings can be viewed by the public, albeit using a good deal of generalized language that prevents their exact meanings from being discerned unless one spends the time to carefully contrast what they have said with what they haven't said to interpolate what they could only really have meant.

The revelation by the Club of Rome that it contrived the idea of using environmental crises to induce people into alignment was undoubtedly a declaration of intent. The future pandemic scenario posed by the Rockefeller Foundation and the pandemic scenario simulation organized by the WEF and the Gates Foundation might be regarded as declarations of intent, as well, especially in light of how interconnected these entities and their interests have been shown to be and the fact that their so-called "predictions" have largely come true.

* * *

"In one sense <u>Magick</u> may be defined as the name given to <u>Science</u> by the vulgar [emphasis added]"

—Aleister Crowley, Magick in Theory and Practice, 1929 [236C]

Dr. Anthony Fauci and Bill Gates have personally made pointed statements that were obviously meant to come across as *predictions*, though they were actually *phrased as declarations*, such as when in 2017 Fauci unequivocally informed his audience in a university auditorium that there would be a "surprise outbreak" during the Trump administration:

> *"...if there's one message that I want to leave with you today, based on my experience —and you'll see that in a moment— is that there's no question that there will be a challenge to the coming administration in the arena of infectious diseases — both chronic infectious diseases, in the sense of already ongoing disease —and we have certainly a large burden of that— but also there will be a surprise outbreak, and I hope by the end of my relatively short presentation you will understand why history —the history of the last thirty-two years that I've been the director of NIAID— will tell the next administration that there's no doubt in anyone's mind that they will be faced with the challenges that their predecessors were faced with".* [237]

In other words —and you must pay *very close attention* to what Fauci's exact phrasing was in order to see this— he was saying that it was *his own professional history* that was the *reason* the new administration *should be sure* that such *problems* would *continue* to arise; as if to say "You know my reputation and what I have done in the past, so do not be surprised when these things occur in the future".

Fauci was not conjecturing when he said that there would be a surprise outbreak during the coming four-year period. He declared it as a fact known to him, and buried within that his choice of wording intimated – whether consciously or not – that he took credit for it.

✲✲✲

Or, consider, when in February 2022 Bill Gates proclaimed "We'll have another pandemic. It will be a different pathogen next time".[238] We have only to wait and see: Perhaps Gates and the WEF will organize *another* pandemic simulation focusing on that *new* pathogen before the *next* breakout occurs.

✲✲✲

There was also the peculiar incident with Professor Sir John Bell, the Regius Professor of Medicine at Oxford University, as he was being interviewed via live stream video by Jon Snow at Channel 4 News on August 24, 2020: In speaking about the status of the development of Oxford's vaccine, Professor Bell exclaimed:

> *"...these vaccines are unlikely to completely <u>sterilize</u> a population. They're very likely to have an effect which works in a percentage – say – sixty or seventy percent We'll have to look quite carefully – and the regulators will have to look quite carefully – to make sure that it's done what we need it to do..."*

Bell continued speaking for a few seconds until Snow —*clearly phased* by what he'd just heard— interrupted Bell in mid-sentence and then just held his hand over his mouth before politely but abruptly ending the interview.[239]

In this case, Bell's later excuse was that he had been misunderstood, claiming that by "sterilize" he had been referring to the effect of immunization. However, even laypeople know that "sterilize" is *not* what vaccines do.

When, in scientific and medical discourse, the verb "sterilize" is applied to a human being as the direct object, it is invariably understood as meaning to render them infertile. For one notable historical example, "Sterilization of the Jewish population of Germany is recommended by the medical counsellor, Dr. Vellguth, writing in the journal of the Hartsmannbund, a physicians' organization."[240]

✳ ✳ ✳

In the WEF's video of predictions for 2030 released in 2016, perhaps the most ominous to my mind was "Western values will have been tested to their breaking point".[241]

That statement is cause for grave concern. "Western Values", although not precisely defined, is commonly understood to include ideals such as democracy, civil liberties and human rights such as freedom of expression and religion.

It is also broadly acknowledged that the people of western nations that uphold such ideals tend to be those that are – no matter what the spiritual beliefs or motives of their founders may truly have been – profoundly guided by underlying Judeo-Christian principles of morality, the sanctity of life and compassion. The WEF's language, vague as it no doubt intentionally is, effectively declares that these values which we hold dear will be opposed until they are destroyed. Therefore, this should be interpreted as *a declaration of war* on those values.

The New World Order

This term "refers to a new period of history evidencing dramatic change in world political thought and the balance of power in international relations. Despite varied interpretations of this term, it is primarily associated with the ideological notion of world governance *only in the sense of* [emphasis added] new collective efforts to identify, understand, or address global problems that go beyond the capacity of individual nation-states to solve. "[241B]

In a nutshell, the second part of the above definition might be paraphrased to say, more simply, that "new world order" only means "world governance" insofar as independent nations rally together (under one standard, so to speak) in order to resolve global crises that they cannot solve on their own.

The gist of the definition is to dismiss anyone's mental picture of a totalitarian one-world government and persuade the reader to envision a more evolved paradigm for humanity where nations voluntarily engage in collective problem-solving for the global common good.

Is it any wonder that the Club of Rome literally proposed leveraging the threat of crisis to get people's hearts and minds aligned against the common enemy? Is it not curious that we are perpetually informed that we are facing one global crisis or another?

Then again, perhaps this is overthinking things. Maybe the mainstream news outlets and the fact checkers on the internet are right, after all, when they claim that plans for a so-called "new world order" *don't exist* or, at least, that the world leaders and diplomats who've been trumpeting it verbatim for decades *couldn't possibly have meant* what we thought they did:

> *"For a new type of progress throughout the world to become a reality, everyone must change. Tolerance is the alpha and omega* of a new world order."*

—**Mikhail Gorbachev**, President of the Soviet Union, during a tour of the United States, June 5th, 1990 [241C] *Note the possibly blasphemous intent in the co-optation of "alpha and omega"; cf. Revelation 1:8, 1:11, 21:6, 22:13.

> *"We stand today at a unique and extraordinary moment. The crisis in the Persian Gulf, as grave as it is, also offers a rare opportunity to move toward an historic period of cooperation. Out of these troubled times, our fifth objective —a new world order— can emerge..."*

—**George W. Bush, Sr.**, President of the United States, in his speech, "Remarks by the President to the Joint Session of Congress", September 11, 1990 [241D 241E]

> *"[President Obama] can give new impetus to American foreign policy. ... I think that his task will be to develop an overall strategy for America in this period, when really a 'new world order' can be created. It's a great opportunity; it isn't such a crisis."*

—**Henry A. Kissinger**, former U.S. Secretary of State, National Security Advisor and Chair of the 9/11 Commission, in his reply to CNBC news anchors when asked what he thought then-President Barack Obama should focus on during the Israeli crisis, January 5, 2009 [241F]

> *"The extraordinary impact of the president-elect on the imagination of humanity is an important element*

in shaping a <u>new world order</u> [emphasis added]. But it defines an opportunity, not a policy."

—**Henry A. Kissinger**, in his article, "The Chance for a New World Order", in *International Herald Tribune*, January 12, 2009 [241G]

"...we can heal injustice by building a <u>new world order</u> [emphasis added] based on solidarity, studying innovative methods to eradicate bullying, poverty and corruption, all working together, each for their own part, without delegating and passing the buck."

—**Pope Francis** (Jorge Mario Bergoglio), Bishop of Rome, in an interview with journalist, Domenico Agasso, published in the book, *Dio E Il Mondo Che Verrà* (translation: *God And The World To Come*) [241H]

"And now is a time when things are shifting. There's going to be a <u>new world order</u> out there, and we've got to lead it."

—**Joseph Biden**, President of the United States, in his speech at Business Roundtable's CEO Quarterly Meeting, March 21, 2022 [241I]

The Christian Bible explains that the final Antichrist —an incarnation or representative of Satan who will be falsely proclaimed as the messiah before the actual reappearance of Jesus Christ— will arise out of an unholy kingdom[242] and establish his governance over the entire world.

As foretold in the Book of Revelation, the final Antichrist will be granted authority over every people, language and nation. His accompanying False Prophet will be able to coerce, by regulating their ability to buy or sell, all who forfeit their spiritual salvation into receiving his mark of allegiance and force them to worship him under penalty of death.[243]

The Latin term, *"Novus Ordo Sec[u]lorum"* (the same printed on the U.S. dollar bill), variously translated as New Secular Order, New Order of the Ages, or New World Order, is popularly understood to be an envisioned system of unified global governance. It is believed by many to signify the global reign of the Antichrist which is expected to commence with the establishment of such a world government.

This interpretation is bolstered by Alice Bailey's Luciferian Theosophical writings telling of an eagerly anticipated "new world order" and a "new world religion" connected therewith. If the name of the United Nations, alone, were not enough, everything we have examined thus far about the decades of influence that Bailey's spiritual philosophy has had on it and its objectives and those of its collaborators suggests this purpose of its existence.

Bailey used the exact term, "new world order", at least eight times,[244] in addition to various allusions to it, in her twenty-four books of esoteric philosophy. Here, I quote from two of those books to illustrate something relevant about the mutually-supportive endeavors of Bailey's Lucis Trust and the appointed executor of the UN's will, the World Economic Forum:

> *"...that will-to-good which has carried all creation on toward a greater glory and a steadily deepening, intelligent responsiveness; this today is creatively endeavouring to bring in the new world order, the order of the Kingdom of God under the physical supervision of the Christ. This might be regarded as the externalisation of the spiritual Hierarchy of our planet. Of this, the return of the Christ to visible activity will be the sign and the symbol."*[245]

In the above passage, from the chapter entitled "The Return of the Christ" in her book, *The Externalisation of the Hierarchy*, Bailey's reference to the "will-to-good" that seeks to bring about the "new world order" is synonymous with both the name of her World Goodwill organization and the particular brand of "goodwill" energy that her network of New World Servers seeks to spread.

Bailey made clear that she regarded the New World Order as the *exposition of the spiritual rulership of our planet* (as for which, it is prudent to refer back to her mention of "The Lord of the World" and to H.M. Blavatsky's earlier proclamation that *Satan* "is the god of our planet"). Here, Bailey also clarified that this epic event will be marked by Christ's reappearance and physical assumption of rulership over this new "Kingdom of God". By having made no allowance for an initial appearance by the Antichrist, she suggested that the false Christ who will initially arise and assume control through this global monarchy will be the true Christ.

In Bailey's book, *Discipleship in the New Age*, she wrote:

> "...*the energy which produces order and which magically brings spirit and matter together (the energy of the seventh ray) is already organising human affairs and these three great coinciding events in time and space make it possible for the seventh ray energies to reach a high point of fused activity and of blended cooperation. The result will be the creation of a direct channel for the precipitation of "light supernal" into the three worlds and its dominant focussing upon the physical plane. Thus will be brought about the new civilisation and the new world order, and the new approach to divinity will be rendered possible; the initial steps will then be taken to create the "new heavens and the new earth.*"[246]

Now, if you will recall what we examined earlier about Bailey's statement that the primary objective of those influenced by "seventh ray energy" of ceremonial magic or organization is to bring about new forms of life, and that this will be accomplished through their working interaction with scientifically-advanced nations, those influenced by the energy of "The Christ", and governments as necessary, it should become evident that the World Economic Forum —that grand organizer of public-private partnerships among governments, corporations, and ultra-wealthy individuals, which is influenced (as seen in its association with the UN) by the Christ of Theosophy (Lucifer) and seeking to make the transhumanist ideal of biodigital convergence a reality— is a prominent working apparatus of the "seventh ray" in the world today.

Bailey suggested that the culmination of seventh-ray energies will bring about the new civilization, the New World Order, and the possibility of a new concept of deity. She proposed that this will be followed by the progressive construction of "new heavens and new earth", which is a reference to scriptures such as Revelation 21:1 wherein it states "Then I saw a new heaven and a new earth, for the first heaven and the first earth had passed away, and the sea was no more".[247]

Here, again, Bailey makes no mention of the reign and defeat of the Antichrist in the meantime between the establishment of the New World Order and that of the eternal state.

Bailey then proceeded to outline the "penetrating process" which she said was necessary for the above. I will only take the time here to point out of a few of the statements she made about this that would be more or less comprehensible to the average person without delving into her Theosophy more deeply than we already have:

> *"The effect of the penetration with which we are now dealing is upon the many varied types of consciousness which express themselves through the seven types of substance."*

> *"The initial act of penetration which takes place 'within the area guarded by the Spirits of the seven Rays.' This connotes extreme activity in Shamballa and also necessitates the cooperation of the Lord of the World and of the entire Council over which He presides."*

> *"Because humanity has passed through a great cleansing process and because in the world today there are many aspirants and disciples, the effect of these penetrating energies is such that they inevitably evoke response. They become polarised or focussed upon the mental plane. Because of this also, everybody who is mentally centred and controlled, as well as aspirationally motivated, is faced with an imperative opportunity. This opportunity is unprecedented in human history and is also based upon certain astrological relationships which I have also touched upon in this series."[248]*

From these statements about "penetration", we can distill the broad and basic idea of a campaign of psychological persuasion, focused on the centers of "Shamballa...Will or Power" (i.e. the centers of authority and influence in the world) and carried out with the cooperation of Satan and his "Council", having the objective of polarizing and focusing public minds on a grand opportunity that must be seized without delay.

At this point, I would like to remind you of the statement that Klaus Schwab, the founder of the WEF, made in the interview in 2017 when he boasted of his organization's achievement of influencing national governments by embedding its Young Global Leaders within them: "...we *penetrate* the cabinets".

"Penetrate" was an interesting choice of a word for his meaning, was it not? One could argue that "infiltrate" would have been more appropriate. As Schwab is a non-native English speaker, though, I suppose that he instinctively used the word that came most readily to his mind for the topic he was speaking about, which was from *the lexicon of Alice Bailey.*

Also recall the statements made in June 2020 by the WEF and, especially, Prince Charles, who used the word "opportunity" to characterize the pandemic three times in as many successive sentences, selling the urgency of the occasion:

"our best chance"

"a golden opportunity"

"unique but rapidly shrinking window of opportunity"

"an opportunity we have never had before and may never have again."

I will reveal a final clue about the spiritual force behind the WEF's assault, if you are willing to see it:

In the WEF's video, at the point that it makes the prediction, "The US won't be the world's leading superpower. A handful of countries will dominate", the background image is a photo of a row of several national flags flying. On the web page where the video is hosted, under the comment relating to that prediction, there is also a static photo of a clearly different set of flags waving on different poles in some other location.[249] However, the one thing oddly in common between the two photos is that they are both centered on flags of *one nation* in particular, which is Turkey.

> *"To the angel of the church in Pergamum write: These are the words of him who has the sharp, double-edged sword. I know where you live —where Satan has his throne. Yet you remain true to my name. You did not renounce your faith in me, not even in the days of Antipas, my faithful witness, who was put to death in your city—where Satan lives."*

—Revelation 2:12-2:13 (NIV)

Ancient Pergamum, also known as Pergamon, or as Pergamos in Greek,[250] was the location of the present-day town of Bergama in Turkey.[251] At the time of John's writing of Revelation, there existed in that place the largest altar ever built to the supreme god of the Greek pantheon, Zeus (a.k.a. Jupiter, to the Romans).

Pergamon Altar, now at the Pergamon Museum in Berlin

The Pergamon altar, in the shape of a three-sided square with a central, gradually inclined span of stair steps, so resembled a massive *seat* that it has —since antiquity— been nicknamed as the "*chair* (or) *throne* of Zeus".[251B]

I believe, therefore, that Jesus was using a reference to this altar in his message to the Church in Pergamum to confirm the true identity of the pagan god, Zeus/Jupiter as Satan.

This notion is given further credence by the fact that Apollo, who is known in Greco-Roman mythology as being the son of Zeus/Jupiter, is specifically named later in Revelation 9:11 as (*Apollyon*) the king of the demonic entities and the angel of the abyss from which they emerge and, I believe, is implicitly equated with the first Beast — understood to be the Antichrist— who is said to have risen from the bottomless pit in verse 11:7.

We may conclude from the above facts that the WEF's apparently deliberate repeated *focus on the nation of Turkey* within the context of its so-called "prediction" concerning what nations will dominate the world by 2030, which we have ample reason by now to interpret as meaning the time by which they and their comrades hope to realize their New World Order, *is a wink and a nod to Satan* in anticipation of his impending rise by proxy to the position of supreme world authority through the final Antichrist.

In 2021, journalist Robert Moynihan interviewed the Italian Roman Catholic Archbishop Carlo Maria Viganò.[252] The Archbishop expressed his views on many of the issues we have gone over here, especially concerning their impact within his Church. I have quoted excerpts of his statements which I feel are most relevant to what has been discussed above (and have also taken the liberty of editing minor grammatical errors).

Although I do not subscribe to the doctrine of Roman Catholicism and by no means recognize the authority of the Papacy as the vicar of Christ on earth, my sense is that the Archbishop is genuine in his faith in Jesus Christ and speaks for many Catholics when he expresses his dire concerns about what is going on with the Papacy.

Especially given his ecclesiastical status, the Archbishop's boldness in vocalizing these concerns is admirable, and Christians of all denominations would do well to heed his words.

In closing, I will leave you to ponder what Archbishop Viganò said:

"It now seems clear to me that we are facing a siege on both the social and religious front. The so-called emergency pandemic has been utilized as a false pretext to impose the vaccination and the Green Pass in many nations of the world, in a simultaneous and coordinated way. [...]

We are at war; a war that is not openly declared; that is not fought with conventional weapons; but a war all the same, in which there are aggressors and aggressees [sic], executioners and victims, kangaroo courts and prisoners; a war in which violence ensues in ostensibly legal forms in order to violate the rights of citizens as well as believers. It is an epochal war that is a prelude to the end times and the Great Apostasy spoken of in sacred scripture. [...]

The alliance [...] is not between State and Church, but between the Deep State and the Deep Church; that is, the degenerated components present within each. [...]

It is obvious the rulers are not pursuing the common good when they expose a population to experimentation without scientific basis, even in the face of evidence of the vaccine's ineffectiveness and the damage it causes to those who have received it; and it is equally obvious that the ecclesiastical hierarchy, insofar as it lends itself to supporting this massacre plan on the global level, is an accomplice to a crime against humanity and – even more – to a very grave sin against God. The Bergoglian Sanhedrin is clearly integral to the plan of the Great Reset; on one hand, because it is pursuing ends which have nothing to do with the purpose of the Catholic Church and, on the other, because it hopes that its complicity can bring it some sort of political and economic advantage in view of the New Order. [...]

We see the ecclesiastical hierarchy – with some exceptions – completely integral to the globalistic [sic] plan of the elite; and not only on the health issue, but also – and above all – on what concerns the Great Reset and the entire ideological structure on which it is based. In order to do this, the hierarchy has had to apostasize the doctrine, deny Christ, dishonor His Church. The Malthusian ecologism, Irenicist ecumenism that is a prelude to the constitution of the universal religion, the "Fourth Revolution" theorized by Klaus Schwab and the family of international finance, find in Bergoglio not a neutral spectator —which would itself already be an unheard of thing— but actually a zealous cooperator who abuses his own moral authority in order to support, ad extra (outside the Church), the project of the dissolution of traditional society, while, ad intra (within the Church), he pursues the project of the demolition of the Church in order to replace Her with a philanthropic organization of Masonic inspiration. [...]

Bergoglio acts on two fronts: an ideological one —with which he wants to prevent any expression of dissent with respect to the failure of the new conciliar path, and also a spiritual one —aimed at preventing the propagation of the objective good of the Holy Sacrifice of the Mass in order to favor those who see in that Mass a terrible obstacle to the establishment of the New Order: Novus Ordo Seculorum; that is, the reign of the Antichrist. [...]

We find ourselves trapped in an impasse – a dead end – from which we cannot escape as long as we do not recognize it for what it is. If we think that the present crisis can be solved by addressing ourselves to the civil or religious authority, as if we were in a condition of relative normality, we continue to not understand that the responsibility for this crisis lays precisely in a betrayal carried out by those who hold authority. We cannot ask for justice for a wrong we have suffered, if the judge were to condemn those who infringe on our rights as their accomplice. We cannot turn to a politician, expecting them to revoke the violations of our fundamental freedoms, if they are the very ones voting for those violations in parliaments, because they obey those who pay them or blackmail them. And we cannot ask the bishops – and even less the Holy See – to protect the rights of the faithful, when bishops and the Vatican itself consider our request as a threat to the power they own and to the bankrupt ideology they defend. [...]

In the civil sphere, there is a need to reject any cooperation with the current pandemic narrative and with the climate emergency that may soon replace it. Disregarding regulations that are illegitimate, that expose citizens to concrete risks for their health, is morally lawful and – in certain circumstances – is even a duty. In no way can one jeopardize one's life or health, or that of one's children – not even in the face of the threat of retaliation. For, in that case, our participation would make us guilty before God and deserving of His punishment. [...]

In no case should be tolerated a pseudopandemic, whose victims are fewer in number than the victims of the supposed vaccines, as an alibi for imposing control and limitation on natural freedom and civil rights; and if the media —as slaves to power and accomplices of this conspiracy— censor every dissenting voice, this should persuade us that dystopian society described by George Orwell is now being realized following a precise script under a single direction. [...]

Those who dissent, that is those who do not accept this turn into Guinea pigs and seeing the world population decimated by transforming it into a mass of chronically ill, must understand that disobedience is just as necessary as it was at the time of other dictatorships of the last century; and, even more so, it is disconcerting that after having built the rhetoric of the post-World War II era on anti-Nazism, no one seems to recognize that the same discrimination that made concentration camps possible is now arising again in a more ruthless form. [...]

Behind the workers of iniquity, there is always and only him [Satan], a murderer from the beginning. It matters little whether the cooperators of this plan are pharmaceutical companies or high finance, philanthropic organizations or Masonic sects, political factions or corrupt media. All of them —aware of it or not— collaborate in the work of the Devil."

Table 4. Vaccination status for individuals ≥12 years infected with Omicron compared to other variants, data included in the table are from 22 November to 14 December 2021

Tabel 4. Vaccinationsstatus for personer ≥12 år med omikron-infektion sammenlignet med andre varianter i perioden fra og med 22. november 2021 til og med 14. december 2021

Vaccination status (12+ year olds)	Other variants (No. of cases)	Other variants (%)	Omicron (No. of cases)	Omicron (%)
Booster vaccinated	6,679	7.3	1,074	10.3
Fully vaccinated	60,174	66.0	8,235	78.7
Not vaccinated	21,364	23.5	947	9.0
Received first dose	2,887	3.2	214	2.0
Total	91,104	100.0	10,470	100.0

Individuals aged 5-11 years have recently been invited for COVID-19 vaccination, hence the vaccination coverage is relatively low in this age group and not included in Table 4.

Personer i aldersgruppen 5-11 år er fornyligt blevet inviteret til covid-19-vaccination, hvorfor vaccinationstilslutningen i denne aldersgruppe foreløbigt er begrænset. Denne aldersgruppe er derfor ikke inkluderet i Tabel 4.

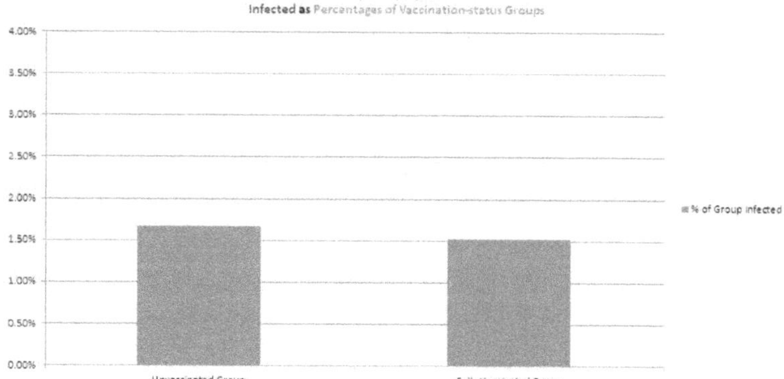

Appendix B

Table 10. COVID-19 cases by vaccination status between week 5 2022 and week 8 2022
Please note that corresponding rates by vaccination status can be found in Table 13.

Cases reported by specimen date between week 5 2022 (w/e 6 February 2022) and week 8 2022 (w/e 27 February 2022)	Total	Unlinked*	Not vaccinated	Received one dose (1 to 20 days before specimen date)	Received one dose, ≥21 days before specimen date	Second dose ≥14 days before specimen date[1]	Third dose ≥14 days before specimen date[1]
	[This data should be interpreted with caution. See information below in footnote about the correct interpretation of these figures]						
Under 18	244,403	11,642	169,482	2,588	40,627	18,961	1,103
18 to 29	197,577	15,845	27,313	816	10,460	54,092	89,051
30 to 39	210,906	12,215	24,469	420	6,525	44,602	122,675
40 to 49	187,850	8,738	13,228	197	3,261	25,954	136,472
50 to 59	144,909	6,562	5,871	81	1,417	12,030	118,948
60 to 69	86,258	3,890	2,263	36	617	4,051	75,401
70 to 79	50,250	2,188	932	19	302	1,501	45,308
80 or over	32,706	2,850	755	7	296	1,807	26,991

* Individuals whose NHS numbers were unavailable to link to the NIMS.
[1] In the context of very high vaccine coverage in the population, even with a highly effective vaccine, it is expected that a large proportion of cases, hospitalisations and deaths would occur in vaccinated individuals, simply because a larger proportion of the population are vaccinated than unvaccinated and no vaccine is 100% effective. This is especially true because vaccination has been prioritised in individuals who are more susceptible or more at risk of severe disease. Individuals in risk groups may also be more at risk of hospitalisation or death due to non-COVID-19 causes, and thus may be hospitalised or die with COVID-19 rather than because of COVID-19.

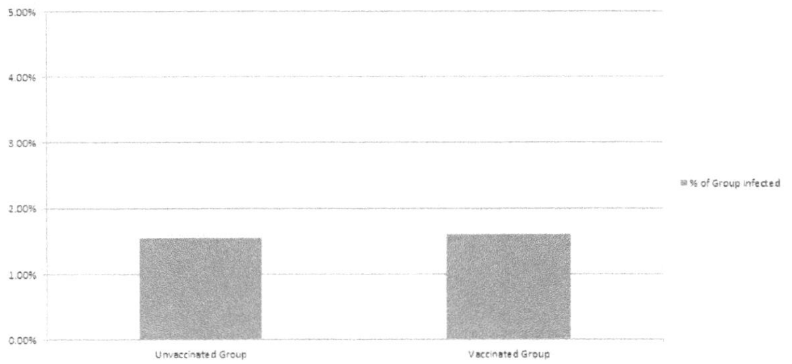

Appendix C

Table 10. COVID-19 cases by vaccination status between week 6 2022 and week 9 2022
Please note that corresponding rates by vaccination status can be found in Table 13.

Cases reported by specimen date between week 6 2022 (w/e 13 February 2022) and week 9 2022 (w/e 6 March 2022)	Total	Unlinked*	Not vaccinated	Received one dose (1 to 20 days before specimen date)	Received one dose, ≥21 days before specimen date	Second dose ≥14 days before specimen date[1]	Third dose ≥14 days before specimen date[1]
	[This data should be interpreted with caution. See information below in footnote about the correct interpretation of these figures]						
Under 18	153,246	7,408	107,498	1,545	21,100	14,758	937
18 to 29	160,211	12,520	21,678	460	8,292	41,070	76,191
30 to 39	172,941	9,758	19,475	233	5,027	33,337	105,111
40 to 49	150,266	6,769	10,400	100	2,461	19,156	111,380
50 to 59	129,112	5,498	4,893	41	1,204	9,595	107,881
60 to 69	81,768	3,315	1,952	19	515	3,437	72,530
70 to 79	48,632	1,904	849	15	266	1,318	44,280
80 or over	31,865	2,666	657	4	241	1,662	26,435

* Individuals whose NHS numbers were unavailable to link to the NIMS.

[1] In the context of very high vaccine coverage in the population, even with a highly effective vaccine, it is expected that a large proportion of cases, hospitalisations and deaths would occur in vaccinated individuals, simply because a larger proportion of the population are vaccinated than unvaccinated and no vaccine is 100% effective. This is especially true because vaccination has been prioritised in individuals who are more susceptible or more at risk of severe disease. Individuals in risk groups may also be more at risk of hospitalisation or death due to non-COVID-19 causes, and thus may be hospitalised or die with COVID-19 rather than because of COVID-19.

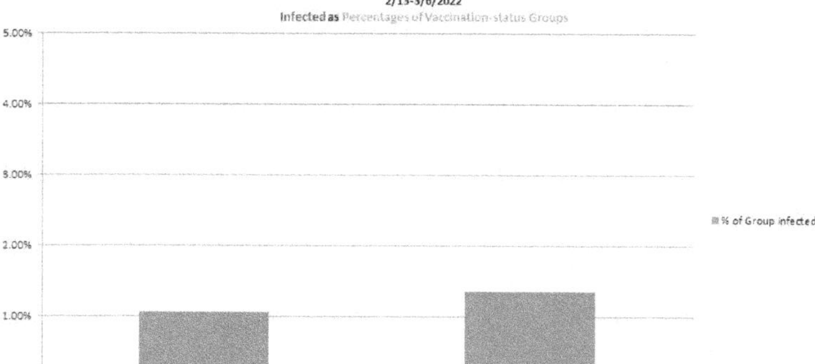

Appendix C (cont.)

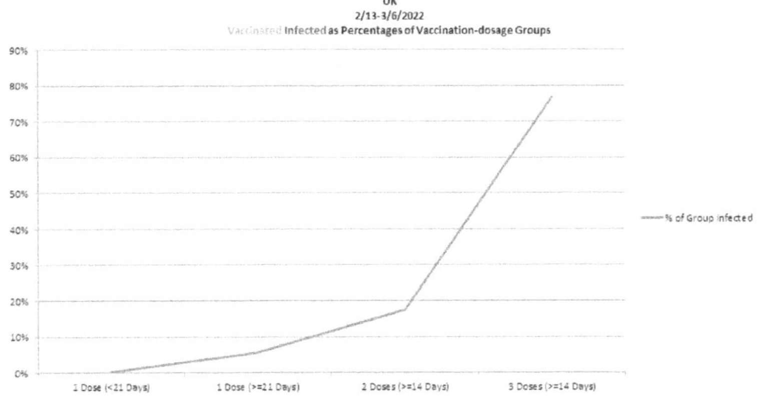

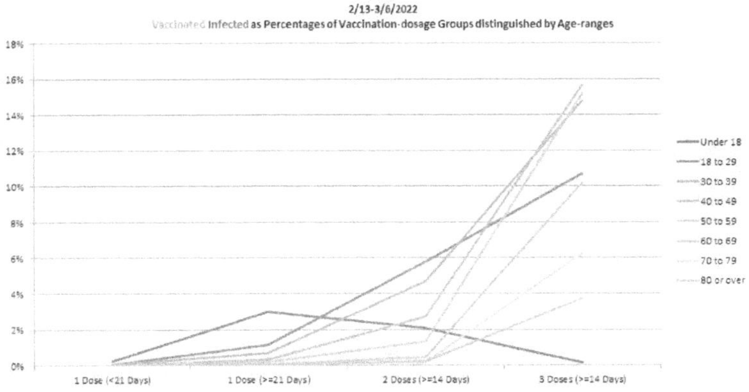

COVID-19 vaccine surveillance report – week 10

Table 11. COVID-19 cases presenting to emergency care (within 28 days of a positive specimen) resulting in an overnight inpatient admission by vaccination status between week 6 2022 and week 9 2022

Please note that corresponding rates by vaccination status can be found in Table 13.

Cases presenting to emergency care (within 28 days of a positive test) resulting in overnight inpatient admission, by specimen date between week 6 2022 (w/e 13 February 2022) and week 9 2022 (w/e 6 March 2022)	Total	Unlinked*	Not vaccinated	Received one dose (1 to 20 days before specimen date)	Received one dose, ≥21 days before specimen date	Second dose ≥14 days before specimen date[1]	Third dose ≥14 days before specimen date[1]
			[This data should be interpreted with caution. See information below in footnote about the correct interpretation of these figures]				
Under 18	734	21	622	9	54	25	3
18 to 29	519	5	142	1	46	147	178
30 to 39	528	2	152	1	41	122	210
40 to 49	502	10	105	0	38	104	245
50 to 59	644	2	113	0	27	124	378
60 to 69	855	2	121	0	26	148	558
70 to 79	1,331	1	118	1	22	133	1,056
80 or over	2,265	0	131	0	35	222	1,877

* Individuals whose NHS numbers were unavailable to link to the NIMS.

[1] In the context of very high vaccine coverage in the population, even with a highly effective vaccine, it is expected that a large proportion of cases, hospitalisations and deaths would occur in vaccinated individuals, simply because a larger proportion of the population are vaccinated than unvaccinated and no vaccine is 100% effective. This is especially true because vaccination has been prioritised in individuals who are more susceptible or more at risk of severe disease. Individuals in risk groups may also be more at risk of hospitalisation or death due to non-COVID-19 causes, and thus may be hospitalised or die with COVID-19 rather than because of COVID-19.

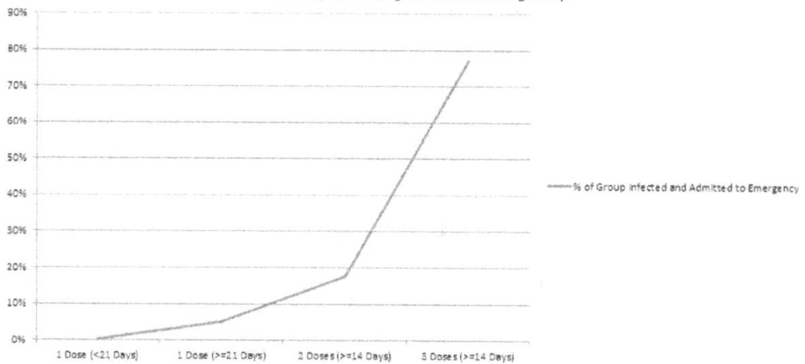

[1]   Big lie   https://en.wikipedia.org/wiki/Big_lie

[2]   The Illuminati & CFR Exposed by Myron Fagan [1967] [Remaster]   https://www.youtube.com/watch?v=RCMmIAWQsIs

[3]   Illuminati   https://www.britannica.com/topic/illuminati-group-designation#ref1250318

[4]   Adam Weishaupt   https://en.wikipedia.org/wiki/Adam_Weishaupt

[5]   3.6.2 Illuminati   https://web.oru.edu/current_students/class_pages/grtheo/mmankins/DrHebert/Dissertation/3.6.2 Illuminati.pdf

[6]   Ibid.

[7]   Alice Bailey   https://en.wikipedia.org/wiki/Alice_Bailey#Lucis_Trust

[8]   Alice Bailey   https://en.wikipedia.org/wiki/Alice_Bailey#cite_ref-Bailey,_Alice_1951_p_1_2-0

[9]   Theosophical Society   https://en.wikipedia.org/wiki/Theosophical_Society

[10]   Helena Blavatsky   https://en.wikipedia.org/wiki/Helena_Blavatsky#cite_ref-FOOTNOTELachman201217%D0%A1%D0%B5%D0%BD%D0%BA%D0%B5%D0%B2%D0%B8%D1%872010179_37-0

[11]   The Secret Doctrine: The Synthesis of Science, Religion and Philosophy, Volume 2, Anthropogenesis   https://www.theosociety.org/pasadena/sd-pdf/SecretDoctrineVol2_eBook.pdf

[12]   The Secret Doctrine: The Synthesis of Science, Religion and Philosophy, Volumes 1 & 2   https://www.holybooks.com/wp-content/uploads/The-Secret-Doctrine-by-H.P.-Blavatsky.pdf

References

[13] The Project Gutenberg EBook of The Secret Doctrine (Third Edition, Vol. 3 of 4) — https://www.gutenberg.org/files/56880/56880-pdf.pdf

[14] Descent and Sacrifice — https://www.lucistrust.org/arcane_school/talks_and_articles/descen t_and_sacrifice

[15] The Esoteric Meaning of Lucifer — https://www.lucistrust.org/arcane_school/talks_and_articles/the_es oteric_meaning_lucifer

[16] Church of Satan — https://en.wikipedia.org/wiki/Church_of_Satan#cite_ref-wikinews_3 -0

[17] The Satanic Temple — https://en.wikipedia.org/wiki/The_Satanic_Temple#cite_ref-Esquire 1_3-0

[18] Satanic Temple Group Raising Money for On-Demand Abortions Echos Satanist History of 'Child Sacrifice,' Says Theologian — https://www.christianpost.com/news/satanic-temple-group-raising- money-for-on-demand-abortions-echoes-satanist-history-of-child-sa crifice-says-theologian-142087/

[19] Support of the United Nations — https://www.lucistrust.org/about_us/support_un

[20] Contact Us — https://www.lucistrust.org/contact_us

[21] United Nations Office at Geneva — https://en.wikipedia.org/wiki/United_Nations_Office_at_Geneva

[22] The World Economic Forum — https://www.weforum.org/

[23] About Dr. Ida Urso, Ph.D. — http://www.isp.aquaac.org/aboutiu.html

[24] Let Purpose Guide the Little Wills of Men: The Spiritual Impulse Behind the United Nations — http://www.aquaac.org/un/impulse.html

[25]	The Externalisation Of The Hierarchy, THE RETURN OF THE CHRIST - Part 1	https://www.lucistrust.org/online_books/the_externalisation_the_hi erarchy_obook/the_return_the_christ_part1
[26]	SERVICE OF THE PLAN, STUDY TWO, Department of Religion	https://www.lucistrust.org/content/download/30682/386749/file/ SOP_2.pdf
[27]	NGO Branch: United Nations Department of Economic and Social Affairs	https://esango.un.org/civilsociety/showProfileDetail.do?method=showProfileDetails&tab=1&profileCode=945
[28]	Support of the United Nations	https://www.lucistrust.org/about_us/support_un
[29]	World Goodwill at the UN Blog, UN Interfaith Week - reflections on the webinar "Uplifting Leadership: inspiring; empowering; inclusive"	https://www.lucistrust.org/blog_wgun/un_interfaith_week_reflectio ns_on_the_webinar
[30]	About the Spiritual Caucus at the United Nations	http://www.spiritualcaucusun.org/about-1.html
[31]	FSV Board & Members	http://ngo-alliance.org/ngo-forums/establishing-a-forum/on-spiritu ality-values/fsv-board/
[32]	World Goodwill: SUPPORTING THE WORK OF THE UNITED NATIONS	https://www.lucistrust.org/world_goodwill/supporting_the_work_of _the_united_nations
[33]	Worldwide Network: Units of Service	https://www.lucistrust.org/worldwide_network/units_service
[34]	World Interfaith Harmony Week: The Official UN Observance in the 1st Week of February	https://worldinterfaithharmonyweek.com

References

[35]	World Goodwill at the UN Blog, UN Interfaith Week - reflections on the webinar "Uplifting Leadership: inspiring; empowering; inclusive"	https://www.lucistrust.org/blog_wgun/un_interfaith_week_reflec tio ns_on_the_webinar
[36]	The Cult of the All-seeing Eye	https://cdn.preterhuman.net/te xts/religion.occult.new_age/occu lt.co nspiracy.and.related/Spenser%2 0- %20The%20Cult%20of%20the% 20All- Seeing%20Eye%20(1960).pdf
[37]	The New Group of World Servers - Key concepts	https://www.lucistrust.org/worl d_goodwill/key_concepts/the_ne w_ group_world_servers3
[38]	A Treatise on White Magic, THE NEW GROUP OF WORLD SERVERS - Part 1	https://www.lucistrust.org/onli ne_books/a_treatise_on_white_m agic _obooks/rule_ten1/the_new_gro up_world_servers_part1
[39]	The Destiny of the Nations 1. The Influence of the Rays Today. - Part 1	https://www.lucistrust.org/onli ne_books/obooks_the_destiny_th e_n ations/1_the_influence_the_rays _today_part1
[40]	Lord of the World	https://en.wikipedia.org/wiki/L ord_of_the_World
[41]	Search Results	https://www.lucistrust.org/onli ne_books/search_results
[42]	Rays and The Initiations RULE TEN - Part 1	https://www.lucistrust.org/onli ne_books/rays_and_the_initiatio ns_o books/part_one_the_fourteen_ru les_for_group_initiation/rule_ten _par t1#master+jesus
[43]	Ibid.	
[44]	Ibid.	
[45]	The World Economic Forum	https://www.weforum.org
[46]	Ibid.	

[47]	World Economic Forum and UN Sign Strategic Partnership Framework	https://www.weforum.org/press/2019/06/world-economic-forum- and-un-sign-strategic-partnership-framework/
[48]	The Great Reset	https://www.weforum.org/great-reset
[49]	The Fourth Industrial Revolution, by Klaus Schwab	https://www.weforum.org/pages/the-fourth-industrial-revolution-b y-klaus-schwab.com
[49B]	What is the fourth industrial revolution?	https://www.weforum.org/agenda/2016/01/what-is-the-fourth-ind ustrial-revolution/
[50]	Gene therapies and COVID-19 vaccines: a necessary discussion in relation with viral vector-based approaches	https://www.ncbi.nlm.nih.gov/pmc/articles/PMC8284696/
[50B]	Bayer executive: mRNA shots are 'gene therapy' marketed as 'vaccines' to gain public trust Referenced Video: "KEY 01 - Opening Ceremony World Health Summit 2021"	https://www.lifesitenews.com/news/bayer-executive-mrna-shots-ar e-gene-therapy-marketed-as-vaccines-to-gain-public-trust/ https://www.youtube.com/watch?v=OJFKBritLlc&list=PLsrCyC4w5A Z8F0xsD3_rzLcfxHbOBRX4W (time mark: 1h 37m 27s)
[50C]	It's Gene Therapy, Not a Vaccine with Dr. David Martin	https://www.westonaprice.org/podcast/its-gene-therapy-not-a-vaccine/
[51]	Nanoparticles in the clinic: An update post COVID - 19 vaccines	https://www.ncbi.nlm.nih.gov/pmc/articles/PMC8420572/

References

[52]	World Economic Forum Founder Klaus Schwab on the Fourth Industrial Revolution	https://www.thechicagocouncil.org/events/world-economic-forum-f ounder-klaus-schwab-fourth-industrial-revolution
[53]	What is the Biodigital Convergence?	https://horizons.gc.ca/en/2021/07/29/what-is-the-biodigital-conve rgence/
[54]	Elon Musk says Neuralink is almost ready to start reading human minds	https://siliconangle.com/2019/07/17/elon-musk-says-neuralink-al most-ready-start-reading-human-minds/
[55]	International Application Published Under the Patent Cooperation Treaty (PCT): International Publication Number WO 2020/060606 A1	https://patentimages.storage.go ogleapis.com/11/a4/fe/095b0d 045 9d9c4/WO2020060606A1.pdf
[56]	Metaverse	https://en.wikipedia.org/wiki/M etaverse
[57]	Exploring Biodigital Convergence	https://horizons.gc.ca/en/2020/02/11/exploring-biodigital-converg ence/

[58]	Klaus Schwab Brags Of Penetrating Most Major World Governments… [David R. Gergen September 20, 2017 Malcolm H. Wiener Lecture on International Political Economy titled "Strengthening Collaboration in a Fractured World" at the Harvard's John F. Kennedy School of Government]	https://rumble.com/vtlk9h-klaus-schwab-brags-of-penetrating-most-major-world-governments.html?mref=lzerp&mc=3ifeq
[59]	The Forum of Young Global Leaders	https://web.archive.org/web/20050730001057/http:/www.younggloballeaders.org/scripts/page8082.html
[60]	Nomination Committee	https://web.archive.org/web/20051029192824/http:/www.younggloballeaders.org/scripts/page8094.html
[61]	Concept	https://web.archive.org/web/20051029192757/http:/www.younggloballeaders.org/scripts/page8089.html
[62]	Health in 2020	https://web.archive.org/web/20051029192713/http:/www.younggloballeaders.org/scripts/page8087.html
[63]	Community | The Forum of Young Global Leaders	https://www.younggloballeaders.org/community?utf8=%E2%9C%93&q=macron&x=10&y=6&status=alumni§or=®ion=#results

References

[64]	Community | The Forum of Young Global Leaders	https://www.younggloballeaders .org/community?utf8=%E2%9C %9 3&q=zuckerberg&x=20&y=9&sta tus=alumni§or=®ion=#re sul ts
[65]	Our Alumni Community	https://www.younggloballeaders .org/our-alumni-community
[66]	Young Global Leaders	https://en.wikipedia.org/wiki/Y oung_Global_Leaders
[67]	Global Shapers Alumni Network	https://www.globalshapers.org/ alumni
[68]	Briefing January 2016: The World Economic Forum, Influential and controversial	https://www.europarl.europa.eu /EPRS/EPRS-Briefing-573928- The- World-Economic-Forum- FINAL.pdf
[69]	Global Shapers Alumni Network	https://www.globalshapers.org/ alumni
[70]	The great reset must place social justice at its centre	https://www.weforum.org/agen da/2020/07/great-reset-must- place -social-justice-centre/
[71]	Global Agenda: 8 predictions for the world in 2030	https://www.weforum.org/agen da/2016/11/8-predictions-for- the- world-in-2030/
[72]	Manifesto of the Communist Party	https://www.marxists.org/archi ve/marx/works/download/pdf/ Ma nifesto.pdf
[73]	Global Agenda: 8 predictions for the world in 2030	https://www.weforum.org/agen da/2016/11/8-predictions-for- the- world-in-2030/
[74]	Welcome To 2030: I Own Nothing, Have No Privacy And Life Has Never Been Better	https://www.forbes.com/sites/ worldeconomicforum/2016/11/ 10/s hopping-i-cant-really- remember-what-that-is-or-how- differently-wel l-live-in- 2030/?sh=5a540da31735
[75]	The great reset must place social justice at its centre	https://www.weforum.org/agen da/2020/07/great-reset-must- place -social-justice-centre/

[76] Stakeholder Capitalism: A Manifesto for a Cohesive and Sustainable World — https://www.weforum.org/press/2020/01/stakeholder-capitalism- a-manifesto-for-a-cohesive-and-sustainable-world

[77] What Happens When Hedge Funds Buy Up Neighborhoods — https://thefederalist.com/2021/06/11/what-happens-when-hedge-f unds-buy-up-neighborhoods/

[78] Why Protesters Want to Defund Police Departments — https://time.com/5849495/black-lives-matter-defund-police-depart ments/

[79] Blackrock is buying every single family house they can find, paying 20-50% above asking price and outbidding normal home buyers — https://www.investmentwatchblog.com/blackrock-is-buying-every-s ingle-family-house-they-can-find-paying-20-50-above-asking-price-a nd-outbidding-normal-home-buyers/

[80] BlackRock under fire amid reports private-equity firms are 'snapping up single-family houses' — https://www.bizpacreview.com/2021/06/11/blackrock-under-fire- amid-reports-private-equity-firms-are-snapping-up-single-family-ho uses-1087586/

[81] CDC Issues Eviction Moratorium Order in Areas of Substantial and High Transmission — https://www.cdc.gov/media/releases/2021/s0803-cdc-eviction-ord er.html

[82] Federal Eviction Moratoriums in Response to the COVID-19 Pandemic — https://crsreports.congress.gov/product/pdf/IN/IN11516

References

[83]	Eviction Moratoria have Prevented Over a Million Eviction Filings in the U.S. during the COVID-19 Pandemic	https://evictionlab.org/missing-eviction-filings/
[84]	Eviction Moratorium Ending, Leaving 8 Million Renters at Risk	https://www.consumereducationcouncil.org/eviction-moratorium-e nding/
[85]	Will coronavirus-induced foreclosures hit Great Recession levels?	https://www.housingwire.com/a rticles/will-coronavirus-induced-fo reclosures-hit-great-recession-levels/
[86]	U.S. Government Covid-19 Economic Stimulus and Relief	https://www.investopedia.com/government-stimulus-efforts-to-figh t-the-covid-19-crisis-4799723
[87]	Value of COVID-19 fiscal stimulus packages in G20 countries as of May 2021, as a share of GDP	https://www.statista.com/statis tics/1107572/covid-19-value-g20-st imulus-packages-share-gdp/
[88]	Saule Omarova	https://en.wikipedia.org/wiki/S aule_Omarova
[89]	'I'm not a communist': Biden banking nominee Saule Omarova forced to defend herself from GOP attacks	https://news.yahoo.com/m-not-communist-biden-banking-1906265 06.html

[90] The People's Ledger: How to Democratize Money and Finance the Economy — https://wp0.vanderbilt.edu/lawreview/2021/10/the-peoples-ledger-how-to-democratize-money-and-finance-the-economy/

[91] The People's Ledger: How to Democratize Money and Finance the Economy — https://vanderbiltlawreview.org/lawreview/wp-content/uploads/sites/278/2021/10/The-Peoples-Ledger.pdf

[92] Biden's 'radical' bank regulator pick Saule Omarova withdraws nomination — https://nypost.com/2021/12/07/bidens-bank-regulator-pick-saule-omarova-withdraws-nomination/

[93] 12 Times Pope Francis Has Openly Promoted a One World Religion or a New World Order — https://www.charismanews.com/opinion/58963-12-times-pope-francis-has-openly-promoted-a-one-world-religion-or-a-new-world-order

[94] The Pope's return flight to Rome: fundamentalism is a sickness that afflicts all religions — https://www.filcatholic.org/the-popes-return-flight-to-rome-fundamentalism-is-a-sickness-that-afflicts-all-religions/

[95] Pope Francis Decrees That Christian Salvation Is Only Through The Roman Catholic Church — https://www.inquisitr.com/1321037/pope-francis-decrees-that-christian-salvation-is-only-through-the-roman-catholic-church/

[96] Pope Francis Calls for Giving United Nations Organization 'Real Teeth' — https://www.breitbart.com/national-security/2020/10/04/pope-francis-calls-for-giving-united-nations-organization-real-teeth/

References

[97]	Pope Francis speaks about abortion and Communion: Don't 'excommunicate' pro-choice politicians	https://www.americamagazine.org/politics-society/2021/09/15/po pe-francis-joe-biden-bishops-communion-241424
[98]	Pope Francis indicates support for same-sex civil unions	https://www.bbc.com/news/wo rld-europe-54627625
[99]	Pope Francis urges people to get vaccinated against Covid-19	https://www.vaticannews.va/en/pope/news/2021-08/pope-francis -appeal-covid-19-vaccines-act-of-love.html
[100]	How public schools brainwash young kids with harmful transgender ideology	https://nypost.com/2021/12/2 2/how-public-schools-brainwash-yo ung-kids-with-harmful-transgender-ideology/
[101]	Critical Race Theory Infiltrates Government, Classrooms	https://www.dailysignal.com/20 21/01/12/critical-race-theory-infilt rates-government-classrooms/
[102]	Why 'wokeness' is the biggest threat to Democrats in the 2022 election	https://edition.cnn.com/2021/0 7/12/politics/woke-green-new-deal -defund-the-police/index.html
[103]	California smash-and-grabs blamed on decriminalizatio n of theft	https://www.washingtontimes.c om/news/2021/nov/24/californ ia- smash-and-grabs-blamed-decriminalizatio/
[104]	California bill would decriminalize psychedelics, paving the way for medical treatment	https://www.theguardian.com/ us-news/2021/feb/17/california-bill -decriminalize-psychedelic-drugs

[105] Why Protesters Want to Defund Police Departments
https://time.com/5849495/black-lives-matter-defund-police-depart ments/

[106] Many police unions are pushing back on vaccine mandates. Here's why
https://www.cnn.com/2021/10/21/us/police-unions-vaccine-work ers-rights/index.html

[107] Federal public servants, RCMP and air and rail travellers must be vaccinated by month's end, Trudeau says
https://www.cbc.ca/news/politi cs/federal-vaccine-mandate-1.6201 528

[108] Analysis | Mishandling of Coronavirus Crisis Is Crushing Young Israelis' Work Ethic
https://www.haaretz.com/israel -news/.premium-israeli-governmen t-s-mishandling-of-crisis-is-crushing-the-young-s-work-ethic-1.9041 402

[109] Minimum wage at $15 would reduce poverty but increase joblessness, CBO says
https://www.bostonglobe.com/2 021/02/08/nation/bidens-15-wag e-proposal-takes-hit-with-cbo-warning/

[110] I get PAID to be homeless in San Francisco - it takes one phone call': 'Old-school junkie' says he moved to woke city because he gets $620-a-month that pays for his Amazon Prime and Netflix and 'cops are like neighbors'
https://www.dailymail.co.uk/ne ws/article-10498607/San-Francisco -homeless-man-says-gets-paid-620-month.html

References

[111]	CDC Issues Eviction Moratorium Order in Areas of Substantial and High Transmission	https://www.cdc.gov/media/releases/2021/s0803-cdc-eviction-ord er.html
[112]	Federal Eviction Moratoriums in Response to the COVID-19 Pandemic	https://crsreports.congress.gov/product/pdf/IN/IN11516
[113]	Farm gates forced open as Victorian government grants access to new riverfront campsites	https://www.abc.net.au/news/rural/2021-08-09/victoria-river-cam psites-open-farmers-angered-government/100361002
[114]	San Diego County wants to build migrant tent city on private farmlands	https://www.washingtonexaminer.com/news/san-diego-wants-migr ant-tent-city
[115]	More than 20 Republican-led states sue Biden for canceling the Keystone XL pipeline	https://www.vox.com/22306919/biden-keystone-xl-trudeau-oil-pip eline-climate-change
[116]	Biden is considering shutting down ANOTHER oil pipeline despite soaring energy prices: Republicans demand Michigan's Line 5 be kept open to avoid a further rise in energy bills this winter	https://www.dailymail.co.uk/news/article-10176399/Biden-admini stration-considering-shutting-pipeline.html

[117] China formalises cut to Australian coal imports, state media reports — https://www.theguardian.com/australia-news/2020/dec/14/china-formalises-cut-to-australias-coal-imports-state-media-reports

[118] Around 160,000 illegal immigrants released into the US since March: report — https://nypost.com/2021/10/13/around-160000-illegal-immigrants-released-into-the-us-since-march-report/

[119] "AFGHAN ADJUSTMENT ACT" WOULD LEGALIZE 36,000 UNVETTED AFGHANS — https://clarion.causeaction.com/2022/03/03/afghan-adjustment-act-would-legalize-36000-unvetted-afghans/

[120] Joe Biden: Voter ID laws "an attempt to repress minority voting" — https://www.cbsnews.com/news/joe-biden-voter-id-laws-an-attem pt-to-repress-minority-voting/

[121] Justice Department suing Georgia over voting restrictions — https://edition.cnn.com/2021/06/25/politics/justice-georgia-voting/index.html

[122] North Carolina court blocks state voter ID law, citing 'intent to target African American voters' — https://www.cnn.com/2021/09/17/politics/north-carolina-court-bl ocks-voter-id-law/index.html

[123] Supreme Court Rules Biden Vaccine Mandate for Businesses is Unconstitutional — https://www.swfinstitute.org/news/90658/supreme-court-rules-bi den-vaccine-mandate-for-businesses-is-unconstitutional

[124] Austria announces mandatory COVID-19 vaccination for all — https://www.jurist.org/news/2021/11/austria-announces-mandato ry-covid-19-vaccination-for-all/

References

[125]	Germany Announces Lockdown For Unvaccinated And Could Soon Make Shots Compulsory	https://www.forbes.com/sites/roberthart/2021/12/02/germany-an nounces-lockdown-for-unvaccinated-and-could-soon-make-shots-co mpulsory/?sh=40c72e0515f0
[126]	Melbourne passes Buenos Aires' world record for time spent in COVID-19 lockdown	https://www.abc.net.au/news/2 021-10-03/melbourne-longest-lock down/100510710
[127]	Toronto lockdown - one of the world's longest?	https://www.bbc.com/news/wo rld-us-canada-57079577
[128]	Inside the world's longest and strictest coronavirus lockdown in the Philippines	https://www.telegraph.co.uk/gl obal-health/science-and-disease/insi de-worlds-longest-strictest-coronavirus-lockdown-philippines/
[129]	Federal government using social-media giants to censor Americans	https://nypost.com/2021/09/0 6/federal-government-using-social- media-giants-to-censor-americans/
[130]	Covid Is Accelerating a Global Censorship Crisis	https://www.wired.com/story/o pinion-covid-is-accelerating-a-globa l-censorship-crisis/
[131]	Videos show Canadian police beating trucker protesters, trampling them with horses	https://americanmilitarynews.c om/2022/02/videos-show-canadian -police-beating-trucker-protesters-trampling-them-with-horses/
[132]	Canadian police seize fuel, remove oil tanker; court silences protesters' horns	https://www.reuters.com/world /americas/canada-police-seen-getti ng-tough-trucker-protests-continue-2022-02-07/

[133]	Woman charged in Australia for inciting anti-lockdown protests	https://edition.cnn.com/2020/09/03/asia/australia-anti-lockdown- arrest-scli-intl/index.html
[134]	FACT FOCUS: Trump, others wrong on US gear left with Taliban	https://apnews.com/article/ap-fact-check-taliban-7adfaa936245d5d 755ec6111c81792c2
[135]	Americans abandoned in Afghanistan as last U.S. troops leave	https://metrovoicenews.com/americans-abandoned-in-afghanistan- as-last-u-s-troops-leave/
[136]	Hannity' on Americans abandoned behind enemy lines, Day 62	https://www.foxnews.com/transcript/hannity-on-americans-abando ned-behind-enemy-lines-day-62
[137]	Rep. Van Drew on Biden's 'bizarre' America: 'I literally feel like I'm in the matrix'	https://www.youtube.com/watch?v=Dij9Si_2Qp8
[137B]	An Encyclopædia of Freemasonry and its Kindred Sciences	https://archive.org/details/AnEncyclopediaOfFreemasonryAGMackeyCopy/An%20Encyclopedia%20of%20Freemasonry%20-%20A%20G%20Mackey%20copy/page/n3/mode/2up?q=ordo+ab+chao
[137C]	What is the Esteemed 33 Degree of Freemasonry?	https://freemasonscommunity.life/what-is-the-esteemed-33-degree-of-freemasonry/
[137D]	Lucifer is the god of Freemasonry	https://amazingdiscoveries.org/S-deception-Freemason_Lucifer_Albert_Pike#!
[138]	Satanic Delco founder on the group's 'To Hell with Homelessness' campaign: 'I wanted us to serve a purpose'	https://www.inquirer.com/news/satanic-delco-founder-joseph-rose -delaware-county-20200909.html

References

[139]	Satanists sue for religious right to ritual abortions	https://www.washingtontimes.com/news/2021/mar/6/satanists-su e-for-religious-right-to-ritual-aborti/
[140]	Satanic Temple to install Sol Invictus holiday display at state Capitol rotunda	https://www.sj-r.com/story/news/state/2021/12/18/satanic-templ e-install-holiday-display-illinois-state-capitol/8952418002/
[141]	'After-School Satan Club' planned at Illinois elementary school. District explains why	https://www.bnd.com/news/state/illinois/article257283327.html
[142]	Another 'After-School Satan Club' is approved, this time at an Ohio elementary school	https://www.miamiherald.com/news/nation-world/national/article 257806878.html
[143]	Manifesto of the Communist Party	https://www.marxists.org/archive/marx/works/download/pdf/Ma nifesto.pdf
[144]	The Fiddler – Karl Marx	https://cbkwgl.wordpress.com/2016/11/05/the-fiddler-karl-marx/
[145]	Marx's Path to Communism	https://mises.org/library/marxs-path-communism
[146]	Marx & Satan	https://legiochristi.com/static/lit/Marx_and_Satan.pdf
[147]	Ibid.	
[148]	Mass killings under communist regimes	https://en.wikipedia.org/wiki/Mass_killings_under_communist_r egi mes
[149]	The Holocaust	https://en.wikipedia.org/wiki/The_Holocaust

[150]	Witchcraft In Disguise	https://www.derekprince.com/sermons/365
[151]	Mass killings under communist regimes	https://en.wikipedia.org/wiki/Mass_killings_under_communist_regi mes
[152]	Book of Enoch	https://en.wikipedia.org/wiki/Book_of_Enoch
[153]	Genesis 6:4	https://biblehub.com/genesis/6-4.htm
[154]	Deuteronomy 18:9-12	https://www.biblegateway.com/passage/?search=Deuteronomy+18%3A9-12&version=ESV
[155]	The Book of the Watchers (Chapters 1–36)	https://ms.augsburgfortress.org/downloads/9780800699109Chapter1.pdf
[156]	My God, what have we done?' - the commander of the 'Enola Gay'	https://www.independent.co.uk/news/world/asia/my-god-what-ha ve-we-done-the-commander-of-the-enola-gay-303774.html
[157]	The Cult of the All-seeing Eye	https://cdn.preterhuman.net/texts/religion.occult.new_age/occult.co nspiracy.and.related/Spenser%20-%20The%20Cult%20of%20the%20All-Seeing%20Eye%20(1960).pdf
[158]	Subversion of the Free World Press - Yuri Bezmenov	https://www.youtube.com/watch?v=sQN4c3uN_tA
[159]	Yuri Bezmenov	https://en.wikipedia.org/wiki/Yuri_Bezmenov
[160]	Yuri Bezmenov - Ideological Subversion. KGB Defector Interview. Call of Duty Cold War Trailer 1984	https://www.youtube.com/watch?v=TEefbbApuaE

References

[161]	Understanding Modern Political Scenario	https://www.youtube.com/watch?v=Y9TviIuXPSE
[162]	Club of Rome	https://en.wikipedia.org/wiki/Club_of_Rome
[163]	The First Global Revolution	https://epdf.pub/queue/club-of-rome-first-global-revolution.html
[164]	1973 - The Davos Manifesto - Building an International Organization for Public-Private Cooperation	https://widgets.weforum.org/history/1973.html
[165]	In Their Own Words: Climate Alarmists Debunk Their 'Science'	https://www.forbes.com/sites/larrybell/2013/02/05/in-their-own- words-climate-alarmists-debunk-their-science/?sh=daf387368a37
[166]	Ibid.	
[167]	WHAT THE PROFESSION OF ARMS CAN TAKE FROM MICHAEL FLYNN'S EXAMPLE	https://mwi.usma.edu/profession-arms-can-take-michael-flynns-exa mple/
[168]	Ibid.	
[169]	In Their Own Words: Climate Alarmists Debunk Their 'Science'	https://www.forbes.com/sites/larrybell/2013/02/05/in-their-own- words-climate-alarmists-debunk-their-science/?sh=daf387368a37
[170]	The 2030 Agenda for Sustainable Development	https://www.un.org/ohrlls/sites/www.un.org.ohrlls/files/2030_age nda_for_sustainable_development_web.pdf
[171]	Climate Change	https://www.weforum.org/topics/climate-change

[172]	Climate Action: 17 Goals to Transform Our World	https://www.un.org/en/climate change/17-goals-to-transform-our- world
[173]	What is the United Nations Framework Convention on Climate Change?	https://unfccc.int/process-and-meetings/the-convention/what-is-th e-united-nations-framework-convention-on-climate-change
[174]	Climate Action: The Paris Agreement	https://www.un.org/en/climate change/paris-agreement
[175]	Climate Action: For a livable climate: Net-zero commitments must be backed by credible action	https://www.un.org/en/climate change/net-zero-coalition
[176]	Fossil Fuels	https://ourworldindata.org/fossi l-fuels
[177]	What is Sustainability?	https://www.sustain.ucla.edu/ what-is-sustainability/
[178]	Scenarios for the Future of Technology and International Development	https://archive.org/details/lock step-rockefeller-foundation/page/1 8/mode/2up
[179]	The WHO and China: Dereliction of Duty	https://www.cfr.org/blog/who-and-china-dereliction-duty
[180]	China Is Avoiding Blame by Trolling the World	https://www.theatlantic.com/id eas/archive/2020/03/china-trolling -world-and-avoiding-blame/608332/
[181]	Dr. Fauci Warned In 2017 Of 'Surprise Outbreak' During Trump Administration	https://www.huffpost.com/entr y/fauci-warned-of-trump-pandemic-2017_n_5e8a0548c5b6e7d76c65 c8a4
[182]	Johns Hopkins Center for Health Security: Event 201	https://en.wikipedia.org/wiki/J ohns_Hopkins_Center_for_Healt h_Sec urity#Event_201

References

[183]	Live Simulation Exercise to Prepare Public and Private Leaders for Pandemic Response	https://www.weforum.org/press /2019/10/live-simulation-exercise- to-prepare-public-and-private-leaders-for-pandemic-response/
[184]	Pneumonia of unknown cause – China	https://www.who.int/emergenci es/disease-outbreak-news/item/20 20-DON229
[185]	How China locked down internally for COVID-19, but pushed foreign travel	https://economictimes.indiatime s.com/blogs/Whathappensif/ho w-c hina-locked-down-internally-for-covid-19-but-pushed-foreign-travel /
[186]	New documents suggest Fauci lied about US-funded coronavirus research in China	https://www.washingtonexamin er.com/opinion/new-documents-su ggest-fauci-lied-about-us-funded-coronavirus-research-in-china
[187]	NEW DETAILS EMERGE ABOUT CORONAVIRUS RESEARCH AT CHINESE LAB	https://theintercept.com/2021/ 09/06/new-details-emerge-about-c oronavirus-research-at-chinese-lab/
[188]	Scientists claim Covid virus contains tiny chunk of DNA that 'matches sequence patented by Moderna THREE YEARS before pandemic began'	https://www.dailymail.co.uk/ne ws/article-10542309/Fresh-lab-lea k-fears-study-finds-genetic-code-Covids-spike-protein-linked-Moder na-patent.html
[189]	Now is the time for a 'great reset'	https://www.weforum.org/agen da/2020/06/now-is-the-time-for-a- great-reset/

[190] Coronavirus crisis presents a 'golden opportunity' to reboot the economy, Prince Charles says
https://www.cnbc.com/2020/06/03/prince-charles-covid-19-a-gold en-opportunity-to-reboot-the-economy.html

[191] The Great Reset
https://www.weforum.org/great-reset

[192] Ibid.

[193] What is Davos? Here's what you need to know about the conference
https://www.businessinsider.com/what-is-davos-world-economic-fo rum-conference-2020-1?op=1

[194] White House team tries to make us believe 'alternative facts'
http://www.workingjournalistpr ess.com/articles/170123/A-lie-told -once-remains-a-lie-but-a-lie-told-a-thousand-times-becomes-the-tru th.php

[195] Joseph Goebbels
https://en.wikipedia.org/wiki/J oseph_Goebbels

[196] Covid: Double vaccinated can still spread virus at home
https://www.bbc.co.uk/news/h ealth-59077036

[197] Covid-19: Rapport om omikronvariante n, 17. dec. | 2021
https://www.ssi.dk/-/media/cdn/files/covid19/omik ron/statusrap port/rapport-omikronvarianten-17122021-ep96.pdf?la=da

[198] Worldometers.in fo View population and growth
https://www.population-world.info/sites/worldometers.in fo/

[199] Denmark Coronavirus Full Vaccination Rate
https://ycharts.com/indicators/denmark_coronavirus_full_vacci nati on_rate

References

[200]	COVID-19 Vaccination in Denmark	https://en.wikipedia.org/wiki/COVID-19_vaccination_in_Denmark
[201]	COVID-19 vaccine surveillance report, Week 9	https://assets.publishing.service.gov.uk/government/uploads/syste m/uploads/attachment_data/fil e/1058464/Vaccine-surveillance-rep ort-week-9.pdf
[202]	United Kingdom Population	https://www.population-world.info/united-kingdom/
[203]	UK Coronavirus Vaccination Rate, any dosage	https://ycharts.com/indicators/uk_coronavirus_vaccination_rate _an y_dosage
[204]	COVID-19 vaccine surveillance report, Week 10	https://assets.publishing.service.gov.uk/government/uploads/syste m/uploads/attachment_data/fil e/1060787/Vaccine_surveillance _rep ort_-_week_10.pdf
[205]	U.K. Population (2022)	https://www.worldometers.info/world-population/uk-population/
[206]	Vaccinations in United Kingdom	https://coronavirus.data.gov.uk /details/vaccinations
[207]	COVID-19 vaccine surveillance report, Week 10	https://assets.publishing.service.gov.uk/government/uploads/syste m/uploads/attachment_data/fil e/1060787/Vaccine_surveillance _rep ort_-_week_10.pdf
[208]	Re: "Vaccine authorities don't really want to know about adverse effects"	https://www.bmj.com/content/357/bmj.j2449/rr-4
[209]	Causality, correlation, VAERS & Vaccines	https://lawrence-robinson.medium.com/causality -correlation-vaers- vaccines-d00af4bb4af9
[210]	Ibid.	

[211]	Search VAERS Database	https://medalerts.org/vaersdb/index.php
[212]	Vaccine Adverse Event Reporting System (VAERS)	https://vaers.hhs.gov/
[213]	Coronavirus Yellow Card reporting site	https://coronavirus-yellowcard.mhra.gov.uk/
[214]	New study: 133x risk of myocarditis after COVID vaccination	https://www.israelnationalnews.com/news/321238
[215]	Myocarditis Cases Reported After mRNA-Based COVID-19 Vaccination in the US From December 2020 to August 2021	https://jamanetwork.com/journals/jama/fullarticle/2788346
[216]	Bill and Melinda Gates Foundation announces $250 million COVID vaccine commitment	https://abcnews.go.com/Technology/bill-melinda-gates-foundation- announces-250-million-covid/story?id=74651890
[217]	Davos, The World Economic Forum, Klaus Schwab & the Great Reset	https://www.clarksvillian.com/post/wef-schwab-davos-global-covid -pandemic
[218]	The Long, Strange History of Bill Gates Population Control Conspiracy Theories	https://www.huffpost.com/entry/bill-gates-coronavirus-vaccine-con spiracy_n_5eb9ab7ac5b69358ef8a9803
[219]	Did Bill Gates Test Unapproved Vaccines on Children in Africa?	https://factcheck.thedispatch.com/p/did-bill-gates-test-unapproved-vaccines?utm_source=url

References

[220]	Family Relationship of Bill Gates and Nelson Rockefeller	https://famouskin.com/famous-kin-chart.php?name=34818+bill+gates&kin=14634+nelson+rockefeller&via=68483+stephen+gifford
[221]	the HUMAN LIFE REVIEW: The Long Road of Eugenics: From Rockefeller to Roe v. Wade	https://humanlifereview.com/wp-content/uploads/2015/11/2004 f all.pdf
[222]	A Conversation with Bill Gates: Making a Healthier World for Children and Future Generations	https://billmoyers.com/content/conversation-bill-gates-making-heal thier-world-children-future-generations-transcript/
[223]	Bill Gates, Eugenics, Vaccines, And Planned Parenthood	http://dean-w-arnold.com/articles-blogs/2020/4/23/bill-gates-eug enics-vaccines-and-planned-parenthood#%5B6%5D=
[224]	American Birth Control League	https://en.wikipedia.org/wiki/American_Birth_Control_League
[225]	the HUMAN LIFE REVIEW: The Long Road of Eugenics: From Rockefeller to Roe v. Wade	https://humanlifereview.com/wp-content/uploads/2015/11/2004 f all.pdf
[226]	Eugenics and Birth Control	https://www.pbs.org/wgbh/americanexperience/features/pill-euge nics-and-birth-control/
[227]	the HUMAN LIFE REVIEW: The Long Road of Eugenics: From Rockefeller to Roe v. Wade	https://humanlifereview.com/wp-content/uploads/2015/11/2004 f all.pdf
[228]	Eugenics and Birth Control	https://www.pbs.org/wgbh/americanexperience/features/pill-euge nics-and-birth-control/

[229]	Margaret Sanger	https://en.wikipedia.org/wiki/Margaret_Sanger#cite_note-Chesler-24
[230]	Lothrop Stoddard	https://en.wikipedia.org/wiki/Lothrop_Stoddard
[231]	Eugenics and Birth Control	https://www.pbs.org/wgbh/americanexperience/features/pill-euge nics-and-birth-control/
[232]	the HUMAN LIFE REVIEW: The Long Road of Eugenics: From Rockefeller to Roe v. Wade	https://humanlifereview.com/wp-content/uploads/2015/11/2004f all.pdf
[233]	Alliance for a Green Revolution in Africa	https://www.rockefellerfoundation.org/initiative/alliance-for-a-gree n-revolution-in-africa/
[234]	Rajiv Shah	https://en.wikipedia.org/wiki/Rajiv_Shah
[235]	Rajiv J. Shah	https://web.archive.org/web/20120419084146/http:/www.wefo ru m.org/young-global-leaders/rajiv-j-shah/index.html?link=no
[236]	12 Biggest Bill Gates Donations	https://spearswms.com/the-12-biggest-bill-gates-donations/
[236B]	Magick in Theory and Practice	https://archive.org/details/b29825064
[236C]	Ibid.	
[237]	Dr. Fauci Warned In 2017 Of 'Surprise Outbreak' During Trump Administration	https://www.huffpost.com/entry/fauci-warned-of-trump-pandemic-2017_n_5e8a0548c5b6e7d76c65c8a4

References

[238]	Bill Gates says Covid risks have 'dramatically reduced' but another pandemic is coming	https://www.cnbc.com/2022/02/18/bill-gates-covid-risks-have-red uced-but-another-pandemic-will-come.html
[239]	'I'm hopeful we're going to start to get readout early in autumn as to whether this thing works or not' – Prof Sir John Bell on Oxford vaccine	https://www.channel4.com/new s/im-hopeful-were-going-to-start-t o-get-readout-early-in-autumn-as-to-whether-this-thing-works-or-n ot-prof-sir-john-bell-on-oxford-vaccine
[240]	Should Sterilize Jews Nazi Doctor Advises	https://www.jta.org/archive/sh ould-sterilize-jews-nazi-doctor-advis es
[241]	Global Agenda: 8 predictions for the world in 2030	https://www.weforum.org/agen da/2016/11/8-predictions-for-the- world-in-2030/
[241B]	New world order (politics)	https://en.wikipedia.org/wiki/N ew_world_order_(politics)
[241C]	Ibid.	
[241D]	Bush Before a Joint Session of Congress (September 11, 1990) - Famous New World Order Speech (time mark: 00h 07m 06s)	https://www.youtube.com/watc h?v=7iUX3yP9M8g
[241E]	1991 Gulf Wars	http://www.cryan.com/war/spe ech/
[241F]	Henry Kissinger: "Obama will create a New World Order"	https://www.youtube.com/watc h?v=q1r-3q9PXoM
[241G]	The Chance for a New World Order	https://www.henryakissinger.co m/articles/the-chance-for-a-new-world-order/

[241H]	Pope Francis: 'We must save lives, not build weapons to destroy them'	https://www.vaticannews.va/en/pope/news/2021-03/pope-francis-book-excerpt-god-world-to-come.html
[241I]	Joe Biden's 'New World Order' Comment Jumped on by Conspiracy Theorists	https://www.newsweek.com/joe-biden-new-world-order-conspiracy-qanon-1690335
[242]	Book of Daniel 7:24-25	https://biblehub.com/daniel/7-24.htm
[243]	Book of Revelation 13	https://biblehub.com/amp/revelation/13.htm
[244]	Search Results	https://www.lucistrust.org/online_books/search_results
[245]	The Externalisation Of The Hierarchy, THE RETURN OF THE CHRIST - Part 2	https://www.lucistrust.org/online_books/the_externalisation_the_hierarchy_obook/the_return_the_christ_part2
[246]	Discipleship in the New Age, Vol. II, SECTION THREE - TEACHINGS ON INITIATION - Part 8	https://www.lucistrust.org/online_books/discipleship_in_the_new_age_vol_ii_obooks/section_three_teachings_on_initiation_part8
[247]	Book of Revelation 21:1	https://biblehub.com/revelation/21-1.htm
[248]	Discipleship in the New Age, Vol. II, SECTION THREE - TEACHINGS ON INITIATION - Part 8	https://www.lucistrust.org/online_books/discipleship_in_the_new_age_vol_ii_obooks/section_three_teachings_on_initiation_part8
[249]	Global Agenda: 8 predictions for the world in 2030	https://www.weforum.org/agenda/2016/11/8-predictions-for-the-world-in-2030/

References

[250]	Pergamon	https://en.wikipedia.org/wiki/Pergamon
[251]	Bergama	https://en.wikipedia.org/wiki/Bergama#History
[251B]	Pergamon Altar	https://en.wikipedia.org/wiki/Pergamon_Altar
[252]	The Viganò Tapes, Dr. Robert Moynihan's Interview with Archbishop Viganò	https://insidethevatican.com/vigano-tapes/the-vigano-tapes/